# IMAGING
# MY INNER FIRE

# IMAGING
# MY INNER FIRE
*Finding My Path Through Creating Art*

## A  MEMOIR
*Martha Jane Petersen*

IMAGING MY INNER FIRE:

*Finding My Path Through Creating Art*

First Printing: May 2013

Printed in the United States of America

Lived and Written by: Martha Jane Petersen

Edited and Project Managed by: Roberta Binder, RobertaEdits.com

Cover and Book Design by: Dana Irwin

ISBN  9780615785936

Additional copies for this title can be ordered through:

www.MarthaJanePetersen.com

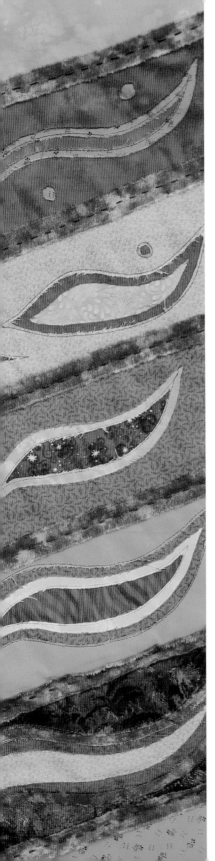

# CONTENTS

**TREE OF LIFE**
49 x 41"

## DEDICATION

### To Pete,

### Without Whose Warm and Enthusiastic Support

### These Pages Would Never Have

### Become A Book

# INVITATION

Who would have thought that my improvisational art making would show me what to do with the rest of my life? In my sixties, an inner fire yearned to be fully expressed, not through words but in images. The invitation to engage seriously in visual art occurred in the spaciousness of retirement. Although flooded with a sense of freedom to make choices, I wondered if I would have time left to cultivate art. At this stage did other more pressing needs and desires require attention? Curiously, it was my quilt-making process which showed me my path, enabled me to respond and eventually to call myself an artist. The pages of this book detail my journey into art.

I make art quilts — fabric wall hangings — improvisationally. This means my creations arise from my imagination, not from quilt books with set patterns, designs, and instructions. In making my quilts, I pre-plan nothing and do not know where I am going when I begin.

When the urge to create a new quilt arises I simply step forward to choose fabrics which seize my attention. In my studio I repeatedly try various arrangements of these selections. Attempting to discern a path without knowing the end result, I trust that I will find my way. I make decisions as artistic choices present themselves. Intuition and a sense of what feels right, plus a swell of energy guides me step by step. The pattern unfolds only as I proceed.

Looking back, I have learned that my life, too, has been an improvisation. As I started out on my life's path, multiple directions confronted me. Through the years, invitations and opportunities have beckoned me to follow. During youth and middle age, various turns and crossroads along the path arose. Faith, logical thought, and outer confirmations assisted me in making choices and assuming various roles across the decades. Late in life, however, a new indicator for guidance arose. The high energy which guided me in making a quilt directed me toward creating art for my later years. I have come to believe that God has endowed me with vigor and passion to lead me into God's intention for me.

**It's the set of the sail and not the gale
that determines the way we go.**

My Aunt Rose copied these words from a popular poem in a card congratulating me upon graduation from high school, more than fifty years ago. I'm not so sure now about the *set of the sail*. I believe that storm-wearied sailors would tell us that gales can powerfully overturn any sea-going vessel no matter how determined the crew may be to go in a certain direction, no matter how the sail is set.

Gales can jerk us off-path, too, as we sail along in life. Not only can they capsize us; they can, as in my case, propel us toward an unimagined direction. My life has unfolded in surprising waves. At one time I set my sail toward nursing. In another era, I determined that writing was the way to go, and squeezed out moments for it around other concerns, chiefly raising three children. At the same time, my husband and I served our church as mission co-workers in Taiwan, Ghana and Nigeria for sixteen years. Then later, a sense of energy and excitement enabled me to hear a call to set my sail toward ordination as a Presbyterian minister. Having responded to God's call, I attended seminary for nine years culminating in ordination as Minister of Word and Sacrament. Pastoral and preaching skills undergirded with theological and biblical assumptions hummed in my bones. I became a spiritual guide and pastor at age 52 followed by thirteen meaningful years of ministry, although tethered to stress, endless commitments and fatigue. When retirement came at 65, I relished more time on my own. I chose what I wanted to do, but always within the framework of what God wanted of me.

With the cracking open of a door of empty time, art came whirling through it. Although art making had popped up sporadically all my life, this time art's insistent invitation jolted me. It prompted me to invest myself fully in art, which provoked an immense quandary over what to do with it. How could a Minister of the *Word* be drawn into image making? Equally jarring was the fact that I had always planned my life by nailing down future dreams along the way, starting at an early age. (In the eighth grade I began to explore colleges and careers, for heaven's sake!) I never relied on improvisation or intuition and so made careful, logical plans. I would set my sail, assuming that no gale would turn me off course. Journal keeping provided insight into the pattern of God's call through the years so I might discern what the next steps might be. God, having created me and redeemed me, after all, has claims on my life. I am accountable. I arduously tried to discern if the invitation to make art — which seemed so illogical at my age — represented a call of God, or a self-wish. Improvisational art making, though, led me, step by step, to answer God's call. *Imaging My Inner Fire* narrates how I responded, built on previous art experiences from my youth onward.

With no history of formal training in visual art, I nevertheless felt gripped by an artistic passion. Even while in seminary I felt compelled to create something with my hands. I longed to play with color. I wanted to visualize my inner fire and to give expression to deeply felt impulses. After retirement I continued to preach, make pastoral calls, and lead workshops and retreats from time to time. Ministry still enfolded me. Once a minister, always a minister, even with no church or office or official installation, I realized. I affirmed that ministry served God and people, but how did art?

Deeply puzzled, questions somersaulted in my mind. *Why this invitation now? What will it mean to accept it? Is God creating in me this passion to create art? Do I have the skills to bring forth meaningful art work? And where does my desire to pursue writing fit in? Does art making comprise God's longing for me? Shall I firmly close the door once and for all on ministry, or could I become a minister-artist?* The questions unsettled me because following a passion for art meant a major turn in the road for me which would consume my remaining years.

Trying to gain clarity about this sense of call, I felt I had wandered into a house of mirrors. I was surrounded by my repeated, probing questions about art, writing and ministry, constantly in my face, insistent at every turn. Their reflections back to me took on shifting, sometimes distorted shapes. I saw in these mirrors parts of the writer, pieces of the artist and an underlay of the minister. First one image would loom large, shrinking the others, and then another would surface in an outlandish shape. Back and forth, up and down and around, leaving me spinning. I wondered how to manage these different parts of myself fairly glaring at each other over turf. I was left on my own trying to assimilate them. This invited insecurity, ambiguity and anxiety.

Right before retirement, I dabbled in art. I experimented with various media: tapestry weaving, paper mosaics, clay, paint on paper, canvas and silk, and art journals and books. I created banners for my church and paintings for my home. But it was in my newfound freedom at 65 that I found my voice as I began to make art quilts. Since then I have continued to create them steadily, in and among pastoral and domestic concerns.

As I made my quilts improvisationally one step at a time, so, in the same way, my call into art making unfolded. I took a step, I paid attention. I saw where to take the next step, both in life and in art. Startling doors of synchronicity and Providence have swung open for me to overcome hesitations, to make and share my art. Walking through these doors, God has led me step by step allowing me to claim my calling as an artist.

This gift of art has served to heal and transform me. It has redirected my life. Because of the privilege to make art I smile more. I pay close attention to nature. My visual acuity remains finely tuned. Furthermore, when I engage in art making, I feel a deeper connection with the Creator. I expect surprises. The energy I have seems to produce more energy. I take care of my body, for I want this venture to last for another ten, twenty or more years. Every day, I wake up overflowing with gratitude to God.

I have written the book that I looked for but never found. Books abound which guide readers through reflections and exercises to enhance their latent creativity. Bookstores and websites also teem with volumes on God's call and on spirituality, even linking spirituality with art and creativity. I sought something different. I needed to hear and to read stories about how the spiritual life has stoked the fires of artistic energy in individuals, how artists discerned their call from God to create art and how they followed it.

*Imaging My Inner Fire* is such a story.

Martha Jane Petersen
Black Mountain, NC    May, 2013

# 1

## PASSION FOR COLOR AND ART

❧❧

## Smitten with Color

A few years before retirement my husband Pete and I enjoyed a sabbatical in California. There, my life turned a corner. When I entered *New Pieces Quilt Shop* in Berkeley I confronted a world of blazing color. Fabrics in swirls, prints, splashes and broad sweeps of solid hues filled every inch of wall space. I hardly knew where to rest my eyes, or where to stop looking. Color was assaulting me but I couldn't help being drawn into it. Every pore of me, every orifice, and every sense lay under siege so that I almost gasped for air. Each bolt of fabric issued a passionate appeal: *Look at me, unfold me, stroke me, get lost in me, and love me.*

Reds bled into each other, some with touches of blue, some with flecks of green, some swept with waves of violet, and others gravitated toward orange or else were overcome in dark shadows. I didn't know the primary color red birthed such a variety of offspring.

Blues nestled against the greens, mingling and mixing, evoking an "Oh!" from my lips. As in the past, the combination pulled me into its tireless peacefulness. I floated as if in the sea with eddies of cobalt blue, emerald and aquamarine washing over me. *I could live and die here,* I thought. *Nothing else matters.*

Moving to the grays and blacks, I discovered an unanticipated liveliness. Paired with ivory and edged with burnt orange, the mélange fairly flamed.

When I placed swatches of yellow and purple, and then red and green, side by side, the complementary colors vibrated and danced. They took on life; they enlivened me.

The fabrics, the patterns, the colors halted my flow of notions, agendas and expectations. My personal geography which tuned me into where I was and what I was doing here in this shop eroded. I had walked off my known maps. Instead, I was smitten with this conflagration of newfound discovery.

■■■

Reeling from the saturation of color, I wandered farther into the shop. Work tables and chairs, sewing machines, irons and boards plus pieces of quilts on the walls peppered the class room. Beyond, a gallery beckoned with an Australian quilter's work. Un-pieced and un-hemmed raw edges marched across a quilt. Another highlighted machine-stitching in squares, spirals and circles. Designs incorporating beads dotted batik and hand-dyed fabrics. This introduction to art quilts engulfed me like music of a great symphony, rising, expanding, and reverberating within and without. I hardly breathed as I wandered around the room. *So this is what you can do with fabric!*

Traditional quilts had stifled me. I sensed a great burden evaporating as I viewed these very different quilts. The only pattern they followed arose from the quilter's imagination, perhaps even improvisation. Now, I could do the same. I could be free of patterns. I could scuttle quilt books with directions and measurements and how-to's. I could abandon the precision of traditional quilt patterns. *I don't do 'straight,'* I told a class once. *I can't measure straight. I can't cut straight. I can't sew straight.* This inability had ended any prospect of making quilts with Nine Patch, Courthouse Steps, or Wedding Ring patterns. No way could I make points come together or corners meet or strips match if I couldn't do 'straight.'

Seeing the art quilts, I danced with a newfound freedom. Possibilities abounded. I could create anything with fabrics and embellishments as far as my imagination would lure me. I would not be constrained by limitations, rules or someone else's imposed patterns. I could work — no *play* — outside the box.

I rounded out my tour of *New Pieces* by returning to its entrance. I noticed a list of classes the shop offered. Starting the next Monday, a three week class would fit exactly into our stay in Berkeley. The clerk assured me that supplies would be provided. I brazenly signed up for *Log Cabins with a Twist*, having not even scissors or thread with me, let alone a sewing machine. Empty of any skill, experience or knowledge about how to make a quilt, I anticipated a dizzying challenge. There was also an undeniable excitement.

■ ■ ■

The first evening of class, we selected the fabrics for our quilt in-the-making. My eyes darted from bolt to bolt. I could not land on any one, two, or three of the assorted, intense colors. Too many lovely choices pulled at me. Too many cried out to belong to me. Too many wanted inclusion in my forthcoming quilt. I had not seen such vibrant colors in southeastern quilt shops. *Only in California*, I mused. I had stepped into a foreign land but thankfully guided through it by our teacher, a nationally recognized quilter.

She advised choosing an assortment of fabrics in different values: prints and solids, darks and lights. Each participant chose her own color scheme. But how, oh how, was I to choose? The blues and greens almost held me captive as in the past. But then my eyes fell on an abstract print of orange, hot pink, purple and red with touches of black. The colors whirled insistently across the cloth and into me. They revved up my energy. They spiked my heartbeat. Still, my wardrobe would never host such outlandish hues. My home décor would toss out fuchsia and orange. Whatever would I do with such a wild color scheme in my life? I hesitated, then screwed up the courage. With determination, I marched to the cutting table with my chosen bolts. *I will not back out of this flamboyant project*, I repeated to myself like a mantra. The scissors sealed my choices.

By succumbing to the vibrancy of the colors before me, something in me had shifted. My choices in life usually derived from well-thought-out considerations. I made plans A and B, probed implications, figured things out, and agonized over pros and cons. I paid little attention to what I *felt*. But here something new, something unplanned and unforeseen had captured me. Feelings overtook logic.

I was listening to my heart.

■■■

It took awhile to conquer the layout of the log cabin block. As if seen from above, the viewer gets the impression of logs built around a center — in my case, a black square of fabric. The *logs* consisted of triangular strips mingled with rectangular ones. The mixture complicated the project. The sequence of construction often confused me.

Gripped with hesitation, I started. I slowly familiarized myself with the class sewing machine. I didn't know what size the seam should be. So I asked: a half an inch? a fourth? My teacher exclaimed, "This really is a first for you, isn't it?" Among quilters, it's common knowledge that seams are a quarter of an inch. I felt like a college freshman, ignorant of the secret traditions of quilting. I swallowed my newness, my inexperience with a great gulp.

At least I knew the basics of sewing with a machine. A tiny increment of skill assuaged my hesitancy. Knowing how to do at least one thing in the midst of a new challenge stiffened my spine with confidence when everything else remained a mystery.

Although a novice to quilt-making, I would not be put off. Something new, something exciting called me. Now in *New Pieces Quilt Shop* I could bear the strangeness of quilt-making because I trusted my teacher who had become my lifeline. With hovering help, lavish reassurance in class and the generous loan of her sewing machine between classes, I was able to complete eight blocks of log cabins before leaving California. With the thrill of this new adventure, I perceived God drawing me into new depths.

## The Untried Path

I carried home the baby not yet full term. The quilt remained fragile in its development and needed more time and work on it before its birth. I protected it, stroked it, and held it close. Nothing could damage it or interfere with its ongoing completion. Familiar now with the pattern of sewing, I finished four more blocks. Next, I had to shape the twelve blocks into a rectangle: four blocks in three rows, connected with strips sewn around all sides. The looming project gave me great pause. I knew what to do next, but could I do it? Cut off from my teacher's reassurance and experience, I felt terribly alone and unskilled.

I tried to staunch the anxiety rising within me. No acquaintance came to mind who could offer help. So I resorted to my secondary resource: books. I turned many pages, book after book. I took notes. I also practiced on sample strips. Finally I geared myself up to finish the quilt and not let it perish. Steeling myself against the blunders I would surely make, I committed myself inexorably to the quilt.

I began by taping the blocks in three rows to my wall. When I looked at the arrangement I shuddered. The blocks varied in size! Would I have to cut some of them down to make them even? Otherwise, how could I possibly sew them into a rectangle? If only I had the advice of my California teacher. Knowing what I know now, she may have even stated that many art quilts don't conform to standard shapes and straight borders. At this stage, however, I was alone with this creature waiting to be born with no support, no reassurance, and no words of encouragement. Just me, all by myself. I felt as if I had been thrown into the sea without a life jacket.

I had to make my own decisions, or mistakes, or — hopefully — come up with an innovative resolution. Trust again was the issue: this time, trust in myself. *Could I possibly pull myself out of this morass of insecurity, take risks, and trust myself to find ways to finish the quilt on my own? What did I need to complete the quilt unaided?* When facing similar challenges in the past, I usually sought out resources outside myself. Now, I knew they could take me only so far. I had to call on my intuition, but I had little experience trusting it. I felt it was hard to pin down and count on it. Still, I experienced an inner knowing, perhaps a sense of guidance. My small degree of intuition told me that I already had what I needed within me.

After stewing over the dilemma for awhile I realized with amazement that I had overlooked another unique resource. They were the colors in the quilt itself. The shimmering beauty of the fabrics, and my eagerness to see them vibrating against each other, fueled my commitment to continue, mistakes or not. Passion for the colors quelled my fears. The colors hauled up trust and courage. Otherwise, I would not have had the *chutzpah* to finish.

## Letting Rules and Reason Fly

Like a general deciding on a plan of battle, I surveyed my options. At first I considered only one: cutting all the blocks the same size. That quick remedy popped into my head first. I soon realized that when I latch on to a single solution too quickly, I squelch a host of innovative possibilities. My nervousness and insecurity make me hunger for quick conclusions. In my hesitation, I had to take deep breaths, hang loose and let other imaginative possibilities arise to the surface. I had to wait. Finding the way takes time.

After a few days, a second option came to mind. I could cut uneven connecting strips and stitch them between the blocks. This would fit the whole quilt into a 51" by 48" rectangle. I wondered if this would be considered a correct solution. But who was to say?

The strips or *sashing*, came from the fabric that launched the quilt — the one with the fuchsia and orange, red and black. It felt brutal to cut into the dazzling colors. To create a rectangle out of the unsymmetrical blocks, I had to cut some of the strips wider than others. That unnerved me. I questioned if this irregularity would pass muster. But irregularity dominated the quilt with all the twisted, angular log cabins. So I plunged ahead with the wide and the narrow strips. *Would the quilt police hound me because of uneven sashing?*

*Had I broken any rules to finish the quilt?*

I pondered this dilemma of rule-keeping over against rule-breaking. There are times any of us agonize over staying within traditional and acceptable boundaries versus coloring outside the lines. Certain projects, visions and schemes occasionally demand launching in new directions. Provocative questions may surface: What rules? And who made the rules? And do rules really matter in creative endeavors?

I think it takes a degree of fierce determination — even a sense of call — to ignore these questions and to follow untraditional paths, in matters of business, community, family or faith. It takes courage and an inner sense of trust, that, *Yes, I can do this in an unorthodox way*. It takes a degree of self-confidence to stand up to real or imagined criticism. In my teens, still plagued with a degree of inferiority, I could not have been so bold. Back then I wanted to swim in the mainstream and not be left shivering on the margins. But now, in my sixties, I let reason and rules fly.

It takes courage to approach new turns in the road. Hopefully, it ripens as we age. It did with me. Maybe courage grows as we grow older when we increasingly disregard others' opinions of ourselves. We respect our own unique sense of direction. We plunge ahead, we make mistakes assuredly. In spite of this we somehow know in God's good Providence and in God's personal workings in our lives, that nothing is wasted, even our limp or screwed-up attempts to engage in something new.

I resolutely cut and stitched uneven sashing. I threw constraints out the window. My quilt represented my first improvisation. I felt liberated and exhilarated. The decision to follow my deep sense of inner directedness felt absolutely right.

When I finished the top I found batting — the puffy layer between front and back — and a fabric for the backing that matched the quilt colors. I thought I should tone down the quilt by sewing subdued colors on the back. The salesperson in the quilt shop steered me toward an outrageous pattern of fuchsia, red and lavender, saying the back was as important as the top. I chose it. Layering the top, the batting and the backing together, I held it all together with safety pins in a kind of sandwich.

## It Is Good

I hung it on my wall. There it stayed, month after month. The next step was to quilt it, that is, sew the three layers together in an interesting stitch design. I figured that quilting it by hand signified hard labor for months, even years. But the thought of putting its bulk under a sewing machine needle for the quilting intimidated me. I had not done such a thing before. Could I manage stitching the quilt without my machine breaking down and myself with it?

After a considerable time, I lurched forward. I didn't draw any pattern for the stitching or make any lines on the top. (Probably only the unseasoned quilter takes such a risky route.) With abandon, I just aimed my machine-stitching toward each block's black center, from one to the other, and it worked, creating diagonal lines all over the quilt. Where quilting lines crisscrossed in the black centers, I sewed a gold bead. I bound the edges of the quilt in purple, made a label for the back, with both the name of the quilt and mine, and date. Making a sleeve to house a rod at the top — like a long open-ended envelope — to hang the quilt completed the process.

I sweated through to the end until I made the very last stitch. There was no more to do with it or for it or on it. It was done.

At the end of each day's creativity in Genesis One, God's assessment "It is good," became my own. In a small measure, I was in sync with God's creative energies, making something out of nothing but thread and cloth, time and imagination. I shared the thrill of having created something new and something unique.

I loved the quilt. I often wrapped it around me and just sat with it, smiling.

Not only was I pleased that I had brought to completion a challenging project, but what I had created warmed my soul. I was awed that the quilt had come to birth under my finger tips.

At *New Pieces* I had seen the words on a T-shirt that verbalized my sentiment: "To quilt is human, to finish is divine."

## Doorways, Not Windows

I called the quilt *Doorways to Passion.* Not only were the colors full of passion for me, but the passion of sewing pieces of fabric into art had hooked me. I thought of calling it *Purple Passion* or *My California Quilt.* But these limp titles could not begin to express the deep shifting within me. The quilt had propelled me into a new phase of my life.

Viewers of the quilt often say, "I see windows in your quilt."

I respond, "Yes, they could be windows. But I see them as doors."

Puzzled, the reply comes, "Really? Why is that?"

"You walk through doorways," I explain. "You have to move. But with windows, you only look through them, passively. Doorways invite more action than windows."

With the quilt I had decidedly walked through a door into a different territory. I had entered a land of imagination, intuition and creativity, a land of life-enhancing color, pattern and design. A new vitality sprang up within me, and I embraced it with a warm, smiling, "Welcome."

For a long time I mused on this decided turn in my life's journey. *What sparked this movement toward art? Why did color vibrate through the cells of my body? Why at this stage of life?* I suspected that the call to art lay long dormant back in youthful years, in Saturday drawing lessons and in sewing my own clothes. Throughout my youth I was captured by visual representation: to paintings and to fabric, to architecture and to nature. I particularly resonated with the sacred spaces of churches, chapels and cathedrals. Then years of non-art intervened while motherhood and ministry engulfed me. With *New Pieces* acting as a catalyst visual art woke up and came bursting into my life.

Then, in my sixties, at the totally right time in my life, a fever fell on me not only to view visual art but to make it. Now was the time to ride the proverbial menopausal energy that launches a woman of my age in a new direction. Now was the time to re-engage lost passions. Now was the time to harvest ripened fruit. Now I faced the genial time of freedom from childcare.

As a wife, mother and minister, I could claim only bits and pieces of time on my own. During those years, I could sew or write a half hour here, twenty minutes there between diapers and dinner, usually when children were napping. I could write or paint for limited periods between parishioner visits and church committee meetings.

Most of us know the constraints of trying to work on a creative project outside the confines of *oughts* and *musts*. We generally consider involvements as frivolous if they do not lie within the range of necessary responsibilities, so we put them at the bottom of our daily to-do lists. Then, approaching that magical retirement age of 65 when I would be solely responsible for the entries on my calendar, time unfolded before me as a beautifully wrapped present. How long I would live and be in command of my faculties, only God knew. Such a time can be a wondrous gift to pick up long neglected projects or to launch into new ones. I intended to exploit my years fully.

With fabric art dawning on the horizon, I perceived excitedly how I would use my time. I would never grow old with this artistic ardor humming in my bones. I would never slide into endless TV watching or talking on the phone to pass the time, or worse, to kill time. For me, God graced me with a gilded gift and I would make use of it to the fullest. I would delight in the days and years ahead, trusting that the way be clear to continue with my art, one step at a time.

I even imagined God smiling when I smiled over the prospect.

# Glimmers

In the ten years prior to *Doorways*, in the midst of becoming an ordained minister, art began to speak to me just below the surface. Only now do I realize the significance of these faint glimmerings.

I recall the ecumenical clergywomen's conference in 1991 at Ghost Ranch Conference Center in northern New Mexico. In the afternoons we had a choice of craft: pottery or making a *mandala* weaving of colorful yarns. Color chose the craft for me since, to me, bland clay pots lacked verve. So I wove a circular design inside an embroidery hoop. With glowing contentment, I handled fluffy yarns streaked with delicious greens, blues and soft grays,

At the same time I designed and made banners for the church where I served and for the Presbytery's conference center. I was commissioned to make a banner for another Atlanta church and a stole for a minister. I made myself a stole of purples and red for Advent and Lent.

I remember two seminars on religious art at the Seminary I attended. Excitement ran high; you could almost palpate the vigor of those weekends. At one, I heard provocative lectures about art and religion by Doug Adams of the Pacific School of Religion. I wanted to take every one of the workshops that were offered during the afternoons: to paint, to create stained glass, to make banners and pottery for churches. At the other seminar, Cathy Kapikian of Wesley United Methodist Seminary led our small group in designing paraments and banners for worship with pieces of lavender, purple, yellow and black pieces of construction paper. We also evaluated the worship space of a nearby church.

The seminars stirred longings to do something visual, something created with my hands, something to express my spiritual vitality. Art making seemed to stoke a fire deep within me. At the same time the inner fire increased the passion to make art. I was discovering that passion has the potential to create end results, and the end results reinforce passion. Around and around.

## Passion

With this new passion invigorating me, I finally looked it up in a *Merriam-Webster's Collegiate Dictionary.* Among other definitions, it defined *passion* as *an intense, driving or overmastering feeling* and *a strong liking for or devotion to some activity, object or concept.*

Indeed, a strong liking, a deep longing for visual art had swept over me which, at times, felt intense and driving. Something welled up within me like a spring — no, a geyser — pulsating to be released. I had no idea why passion in the guise of art had invaded my life, or where it would lead. *Would it mean sitting in solitary splendor, reveling in color and fabric as I made quilts while the rest of the world fell apart?*

Early on, this question was barely beginning to penetrate my awareness. Prior to my *Passion* quilt, I remember looking through a pile of vividly printed fabrics I had brought home from Africa. I caressed the pieces. I imagined what I could do with them. I longed to work with them in some way. With this longing, however, I realized a possible detour from ministry. *Would quilting lead me away from serving others? How does a sewing room fit into ministry? Would I still be considered a pastor? Could this be an extraordinary ministry recognized by my church?* The questions would take time to unravel and resolve their complexities.

I put the fabrics back in the closet and closed the door. For now, I decided art making belonged in extracurricular storage units of optional things to do. Like hobbies. I had thought the closing of that door was final. But then *Doorways to Passion* tested my limits and understanding.

With the freedom and time to make my first quilt, the longings could not be denied. Through this art form I was coming alive. A new energy coursed through my veins. Passion had opened its door to me and I had walked through it. The questions about art and ministry took on new force.

I began to examine passion in my life from childhood onward. What had captured me? Beginning about age thirteen, I gravitated toward the things of God and the will of God. In the labyrinthine twists and turns of my childhood and youth, God touched my life. I had responded with the words of the hymn: *Teach me to love Thee as Thine angels love: one holy passion filling all my frame... my heart an altar and Thy love the flame.* Love's flame was personified in Christ Jesus, the ultimate focus of my heart's passion.

Through Bible teachers, youth advisors, church educators, ministers and peers, I grew. I prayed, studied the Bible and shared faith with others. I longed to convey what God meant to me, to proclaim the Good News of God's love. That represented my purpose in life, my mandate, my commission which resulted in a call to serve my church overseas as a mission co-worker and to become an ordained minister when we returned home. If I engaged in art making, though, would my passion for God and my sense of mission grow brighter or dimmer?

I explored *passion* in a dozen contexts. In Joseph Campbell's *The Power of Myth,* I found his notion of *bliss* and equated it with passion. I resonated with his words. From time to time, he said, life will show us where our bliss lies. When that happens, he admonished:

> *Grab it. No one can tell you what it's going to be. You have to learn to recognize your own depth.... If you follow your bliss you put yourself on a kind of track that has been there all the while waiting for you, and the life that you ought to be living is the one you are living. When you can see that, you begin to meet people in the field of your bliss, and they open doors to you... doors will open where you didn't know they were going to be.*

I was definitely on a kind of track. Doors had begun to fly open that I didn't know existed. Contacts at social gatherings, opportunities to view galleries or attend art retreats, avenues to share my beginning passion for art all fell into my lap. As a friend said to me, "You're not just talking about 'open doors.' You're talking about doors crashing wide open without even a movement from you!" I detected Providence behind the openings.

One such door opened when I was invited to teach two adult Sunday classes about art at a nearby church. New in the field of artistic interests, I cannot remember how the invitation came about. I was astonished and flattered. The first Sunday I taught what happened to art in Protestant churches and why we need it. For the second session, I brought several examples of banners from different churches in Atlanta. I had the class evaluate them. I stressed my conviction that banners needed no words on them. "Visual art such as banners in a sanctuary should stand on its own" I explained. "Art is an alternative way of accessing the Holy ... beyond the many, many words used in a worship service."

The class paid very close attention. When I finished the second session, they rose to their feet and gave me an extended round of applause.

Ellen Phillips, the class member who had invited me, wrote in a thank you letter: "Your lesson was provocative, interesting, stimulating and a lot of other words that still couldn't sum up how much we got from you. Let me just put it this way: never, never in the history of our seventeen year-old class has *anyone* received an ovation! You are in your calling and God is using you in a wonderful way."

I was floored. What really came across in the class? What did I do to evoke such a response? Apparently my passion clearly revealed itself. And what did Ellen mean about my "calling?" Was it simply to unveil my passion about art? And did a calling lie before me that I couldn't see but others could? Did my longing to make art constitute a "call?"

The only thing I could claim at that point was my new and burning passion. Where would it take me? I needed to know what lay ahead. Even though I wanted to stay open, to hang loose, to rely on trust, I needed assurance to know if art was the path God wanted me to take. I needed to know: *if I really followed my bliss would it lead me closer to God, or lead me away?*

Yes, I longed to follow God's leading, not mine. I wanted to give God pleasure. I wanted to be in sync with God's desires and plans for me, believing that God truly had my well-being at heart. From adolescence I committed myself to aligning my life with God's will. Not out of fear or ought or guilt. But out of love. Out of a relationship with God through knowing his Son who has companioned me and opened me to life's depths. I have hosted countless longings, but have learned that fundamentally my deepest longing is for God.

Questions and more questions tumbled over each other. I meekly trusted that, as Rilke says, "I would live along some distant day into the answer."

I pondered my questions as I showed the *Passion* quilt to my spiritual guide, Sister Loretta. For about two years, I had been meeting monthly with Loretta, seeking the direction of God's Spirit for my life.

"Should I do art or not?" I urgently asked.

She wisely skirted my demanding question, waiting for me to find my own truth. She remarked that art was giving me life and she did not believe that anything that would create vitality in a soul would not be of God. She noted how my demeanor changed when I spoke of art and when I described the process of making the quilt. "You become more lively," she said. "And when you show your quilt you show the new you that is emerging. That is part of this gift. God *may* be doing art through you, but God is certainly doing *you* through art."

**DOORWAYS TO PASSION**
49 x 41"

*"I often wrapped the quilt around me
and just sat with it, smiling."*

# 2
## CULTIVATING A VISION

❧

### Art Making As A Call

As I contemplated the new open door in my life I found it vast, wondrous and intimidating. The art world stretched before me in countless variations. With every sense finely tuned to receive all in-coming stimuli — to pay attention — I pictured myself on a mountain top, looking out over a sweeping valley full of potential. Without trying to pinpoint a specific road to travel, or a defined point of entry, I simply basked in the thought of exploding possibilities. But sooner or later, I needed to know what to do next. I needed a vision to direct me.

Before leaving for that three-month sabbatical in California, my friend Connie Conrad asked me, "What will you do there?" I replied, "Explore art and absorb everything." So I sought visits with artists, exhibitions, conferences plus hands-on opportunities to engage in art making where possible.

Friends in San Anselmo, CA encouraged me to contact Nancy Chinn, a nationally known liturgical artist. Eager to meet her, I nevertheless expressed my timidity about walking up to her door and saying "I'd like to talk with you." My friends said that Nancy treasured mentoring budding artists. They gave me her phone number and insisted I call her. Mustering up nerve, I did.

Nancy had just finished teaching a course at the Pacific School of Religion, entitled *Art Informing Faith*. The link of art with faith rang in my ears. The students had mounted an exhibition of their work. It stunned me. Not only did the show make visible the spiritual life of the student-artists, but also the pain of the women who dominated the class. In the artwork, they expressed the discrimination, abuse and neglect they had suffered through the garish colors and sweeping strokes on large pieces of paper. I gazed and gazed at the images hanging on the walls. Their renditions spoke volumes. The artists' statements described increments of healing by expressing their anguish through art.

I met Nancy at the exhibition and she invited me to her home a few days later. We met for four significant hours. During the first two hours she showed me her paintings on her walls and in her slides. She had painted a series entitled *Even the Stones Cry Out*. They depicted the lives of biblical marginalized women: Hagar, Susanna, Dinah, Jephthah's daughter, and several others. The colors and arrangements of design vibrated. They, too, depicted the pain of women.

We then talked about art books and exhibitions that might be helpful for me. The notion of *kitsch* (the cute, sentimental and banal), and how to avoid it. Then the *numinous* in art, in which viewers experience a holy presence in the piece.

She introduced me to Bezalel. "Do you know Bezalel?" She asked.

"No," I responded. "Who's he?"

She found a Bible and read a remote biblical story about the Hebrew people building and decorating the tabernacle, the portable sacred space for worship of God which they carried with them on their journey through the wilderness.

> And Moses said to the Israelites, "See, the Lord has called by name Bezalel ... And [God] has filled him with divine spirit, with skill, intelligence, and knowledge in every kind of craft, to devise artistic designs to work in gold, silver, and bronze, in cutting stones for setting, and in carving wood ... [and to work with] blue, purple and crimson yarns and in fine linen.... Moses then called Bezalel and Oholiab and every skillful one to whom

the Lord had given skill, everyone whose heart was stirred to come to do the work...."

Exodus 35:30-33; 36:2

Nancy put the Bible down, and looked at me. She didn't say anything. She just let the words sink in.

I sat there in a daze trying to grasp the meaning of what I had heard. I had never known about this multi-talented Bezalel, hidden away in a rarely read passage of Scripture. I couldn't take in all the arts and crafts done by designers, setters of stones, carvers of wood, and weavers and embroiderers. The colors "blue, purple, crimson yarns" tingled in the air, and danced in my heart. And "skill," "mind," and a "stirred heart" swirled in my mind.

Finally I said, "You mean, God called persons to make all this art?"

She nodded mutely.

The passage of Scripture told me that God loved beautiful works of art; that God called people by name to make art; that the divine Spirit of God gave artists the skills to create; and that a stirring of the heart accompanied both the call to the work and the ability to do it.

There it was: call, a filling of the Spirit, skill and passion all wrapped together. All from God. *All because of God's desire for beautiful art.* I could hardly absorb the thought that artists — not just prophets and apostles — were called personally by God. Not only that, they were filled with the Spirit to do their work. (Was it ever mentioned that Moses was "filled with the Spirit"?) I shook my head in wonder.

I then asked Nancy, "Why should God invest in artistic beauty?"

"Because God dwells in beauty! Plus art can reach people, and touch their lives in unique ways — beyond words, beyond thoughts."

"So... art can be a ministry?" I stumbled for words. She nodded.

I saw art in a whole new light. Understandings surfaced and marched across my mind:

- God's agenda includes art and art making.

- Artists' beautiful, or even disturbing, creations can draw people to the Holy One.

- Beauty expressed in art acts as a lure to God.

- Art poses questions about life and death, about faith and spirituality.

- As a ministry, making art transmutes from being a mere pastime or a hobby to constitute a life's devotion.

- A call from God to create art cannot be ignored.

Thank God for Bezalel. A burden rolled off me. With a mixture of both unease and passion, I had gravitated toward paintings, color, fabrics and artists of skill and imagination. If God were calling me to do art, then this gravitation, this pull was legitimate. Of course, I had been pulled in the direction of ministry also. I perceived no way of discounting that call. And as a minister, was I steering off course from what I was ordained to do, as Minister *of the Word?* That posed the source of my discomfort. Now, with Bezalel, a new insight crossed my path. I saw his art serving God. I saw in him a ministry. But would some form of art making be part of *my* ministry? Could I be both a minister and an artist?

At lunch, I spread these questions on the table around our Mexican burritos and enchiladas. She kept coming back to Yes, art can be a ministry. As to whether it was my ministry, "Just be open — and keep exploring," Nancy said.

After lunch, we talked some more. Nancy posed four pivotal questions followed by my tentative answers.

She asked, "What is your present greatest vision in your art?"

Hesitantly, I responded. "I'd like to be able to share something of God through art."

"What do you mean? Can you be more specific?"

After some pause, I said, "To share visually something that provokes and nourishes the spiritual life of persons... something of mystery ... and quest."

"Perhaps you mean...the numinous in art?

"That's it ... exactly."

"What is the first step you need to take to achieve your vision?"

I immediately knew. "To acquire some space for work."

I told Nancy of the cramped space I had been working in: a corner of my rather dark study in our apartment. But now our daughter was moving out, leaving a bedroom free. Nancy helped me to visualize setting it up. I named its source of light and water — the big window, and the bathroom's water only steps away. We also talked about what basic skills I needed to learn. "Probably not from classes," she said, "more from an individual teacher, or mentor." I thought of one or two in the Atlanta area.

Then Nancy asked, "What is one fear that is related to this process?"

"That nothing would come of this," I said. "That I would have little to show from my call and for my efforts. That lots of self-doubts would plague me, and I'd be constantly asking myself: why am I ordained? That, if I go off on this crazy artistic tangent, maybe my ordination would even become invalid in the eyes of the church."

"A fear that self-doubt and others' opinions would make you forget and be distracted from what you know?"

"Yes," I said.

Lastly she asked, "So what kind of help do you need to stay on track? What would that 'help' look like?"

"Someone to listen to me, to guide me, to affirm me...like you have."

"Are there some in Atlanta who could fill this need?" she asked.

I responded with the names of Sara, Connie, another friend — Anne, and Sister Loretta.

"Would a ritual of some kind help launch you in this direction?"

"Yes, possibly."

Then Nancy added, "Remember, Martha Jane, when you entered seminary you did not know where it would lead. Nothing was crystal clear when you began. The same here. Your future in art may remain elusive for a time. Just take one step at a time, and the way forward will become clear as you go along."

I left Nancy with my head swimming. Pete waited for me in the car. I hesitated to tell him about my visit with Nancy.

Just weeks before, back home, I had remarked that I'd like to do more with art. He had said, "Paint pictures? Make quilts? Do what? "

"I'm trying to figure it all out," I responded.

He lifted his eyes from the book he was reading, and chuckled. "Well, honey, I'd like to play with model trains, too!"

I had climbed out of that crushing statement the best I could. I didn't know what to say or how to express my quandary. Perhaps, confused as I was, I should have refrained from speaking until the muddy water had cleared. I viewed art as far more than a hobby, but a calling? A ministry? What?

Now he waited in the car to hear what I had gleaned from Nancy. How would he react? When I told him, he surprisingly and enthusiastically supported me. "We must make you a headquarters!" he said. We then re-imagined the newly vacant room in our apartment with work space for art. He laid out a better design for the space than I had envisioned.

It was the beginning of Pete's dedicated support in my growth as an artist. Through the years, he has encouraged me to attend workshops, agreeably paying their fees and staying at home alone. He has never begrudged my purchases of fabric and books. He has supported me by holding up my quilts when I explain them to groups of people, and has even organized such groups to see my quilts. He has viewed my work on display at every exhibition. He has driven me to far flung destinations to view others' art. He arranged a studio for me in our retirement home without my asking for it. I could not ask for more.

After we talked, I went to a stationery store to look for a journal. It had to have a beautiful cover and unlined paper. I found the perfect one. I wrote on the first page a title: "Nurturing the Vision," and recorded the conversation with Nancy. I would continue to write and paste in it scraps of quotes about art, objects from nature, and prints. It would help me stay on track and subdue doubts. And not to forget what I knew, from that day onward.

I walked tall that day, sensing God taking me by the hand. Whether art as ministry lay in my future or not, I had confidence that God would lead me, one step at a time. I would discover my path as I walked it.

## People in the Field of My Bliss

After seeing Nancy, I visited with quilt artist, Holly Junker, in Sacramento. I had seen one captivating piece of her work in an issue of *Fiberarts* magazine before leaving home. The magazine mentioned that she had exhibited her work at a North Carolina college. I wrote the college for any materials relating to the exhibition, and to find out her address in California. Amazingly, the college forwarded my letter to her, and she responded with an invitation to come see her. "Artists are only too glad when someone notices their work. We are more than happy to show it to anybody interested in it," she explained when, at her door, I apologized for my intrusion.

Her home and garden resembled a photo out of *House Beautiful.* Her studio seemed to have morphed from a kitchen and dining area, with ample table space and sink. Finished pieces and works in progress hung on her walls. I immediately went to the quilt that had been pictured in *Fiberarts.* I gazed intently at it, observing her design and technique. She had cut out coin-shaped pieces of fabric in nuanced hues and "painted" a scene with them. "What an innovative idea," I remarked. After my tour of her work, we talked animatedly about designs and methods. Viewing the colors and images before me, a surge of passion drummed in my veins.

Visiting her, however, raised deep questions. On the surface, she seemed isolated, withdrawn from the cares of the world to create her stunning quilts in serene surroundings. Perhaps she engaged in other activities beyond the perimeters of her lush lawn. Perhaps she even created her art to benefit marginalized people. Who was I to judge? In whatever way Holly may have connected her art with social needs, her home and studio caused me to ask: *Do I have to withdraw like a recluse to do art? Do I have to turn my back on the world's pressing needs?* Those insistent questions sharply prodded me.

Still, when I left her, I stayed on course. I went to a nearby fabric store and bought some yardage. For what project I had no clue. Certain pieces simply pulled me toward them. It was the beginning of my quilter's stash.

Later, I attended an art, creativity and spirituality conference at Grace Episcopal Cathedral in San Francisco. About 300 people crowded in to hear keynote speaker, Meinrad Craighead, a visionary painter from New Mexico. At the break, we picked up our box lunches and then scattered to various places to eat. I found myself knee to knee with the woman who had been sitting next to me in the meetings. In a small park opposite the cathedral, Penelope Starr and I ate together and shared details about our lives.

"I can't figure out something," I said, "Why am I ordained as a Presbyterian minister to do art? Why didn't I get a Masters in Fine Arts degree instead?"

"Do you want to do art in the church?"

"I'd love to."

"Your being a minister will be essential if you want to do art in the church. Your credentials are no small thing."

We chewed and we drank in silence for awhile. Then, "Why should I be called to do this at this stage in my life — nearing sixty?" I asked.

Penelope related the story of her mother who had told her children that when all of them were out of the nest, she would "sprout wings and fly." Her mother started a career in photography at age 60 and it lasted for 20 years. That story became a permanent deposit in my memory bank.

I said, "All my peers are deep into their careers, their callings. But look at me — still not knowing what I'm going to be when I grow up!"

"Don't compare yourself with women your age," she said. "You're more at the level of a 25 year-old, fresh out of grad school. And it's *OK to be there*."

Then I listened to her challenge. She made glass and metal water fountains — they were the love of her life. She had one last child to get through college, and she had to work full-time in a glass company for the tuition. It looked as if Penelope couldn't live out her passion for another four years. She spread out her hands in a gesture of helplessness.

I told her about my "Nurture the Vision" journal and about my visits with artists. "You need something to keep your dream alive," I said. We talked about how this could happen. We discussed various options for funding and arrangements for her to do her art along with supporting her daughter.

We finished our lunch when the meetings reconvened. Incredibly, out of the random selection of persons to sit with during lunch, Providence must have brought us together. The support we gave to each other in that short hour simply astonished me.

I was further astonished that afternoon in a workshop when we drew an improvisational image in a mandala with white chalk on black paper. A horse and rider in moonlight emerged and surprised me. I sensed the drawing say to me, *Now get on your horse and ride it!*

I later went to see Penelope in her home studio. I saw her passion, vibrating in glass — sheets and shards, dust-covered tables and floor interspersed with all sorts of strange looking tools, pieces of metal framing, soldering and glass cutting machines. A shimmering stained glass window made by her hung high above the chaos. She showed me photos of her fountains. She exuded pleasure and energy as we talked.

"Keep living the dream — at all costs," I said.

■ ■ ■

For a few days, Pete and I had the privilege of using a friend's vacation house on the beach at Bolinas, a small town north of San Francisco. Dazzling sunlight ricocheted from sand and surf right up to the deck of the house. To the north, trees hovered over the sand like giant birds; the lights of San Francisco twinkled at dusk from the south. At night, the ocean's booming against the house sounded downright threatening. *Did we need to bed down with life jackets since we might be swept out to sea by daybreak?* Between the breakers, I could hear the surf humming. It rolled into me and set me singing. It connected me with God's beautiful creation.

Pentecost and Mothers' Day came while we lolled in Bolinas. I took a long walk up the hill behind us. Eucalyptus trees shaded the lane. Their pungent scent enfolded me. Teeming nasturtiums in yellows, golds and reds cascaded down rock walls sometimes intertwined with bright blue morning glories. At the top of the hill, I could view the vast stretch of sea, glinting in the mid-day sunlight.

Energy and joy flooded me. The vivid colors invaded and nourished me from the depths. I collected nasturtium and morning glory blossoms, a stem of wheat, a eucalyptus leaf and another leaf shot through with gold. I spent a long time sitting on a wall, and gazing at nature in her glory. I also smiled.

Upon returning to the house, I wrote in my "Vision" journal:

*I feel a new fecundity,*
*A new creation about to be birthed.*
*The seed lies dormant, but it has been planted —*
    *It's there, by God's grace!*
*But it awaits in a gestational state,*
*Waits for the fiery, energizing Spirit to bring life,*
*To spark it into growth and flowering.*
*How appropriate that mothering and Spirit should be*
    *So closely approximated on the calendar*
    *And in real life!*
*Impregnated by the Spirit,*
*Quickened by the Spirit,*
*Birthed, brought forth, delivered by the Spirit*
*The trusting, accepting woman*
*Becomes the new mother*
*The creative mother*
*Even the mother past her prime!*

■ ■ ■

I pasted the leaves and flowers in my new journal and attached meanings to them. The eucalyptus leaf represented: energy and passion; the morning glory: God's faithfulness, new every morning; the wheat: fruitfulness; the nasturtium: joy, and the gold leaf symbolized transcendence and glory.

Clearly, I was in a waiting period to see which way to go. Later, a friend sent a card to me with the image of an angel pointing down a hallway at the end of which was a dark, partly opened door. I wrote in my journal:

*Angel, angel, what do you point to?*
    *Through the hall, down the hallway*
*Stands an open door —*
    *Black, empty, open;*

*What lies there?*
*What turns do I take?*
*You're pointing, pointing*
*And I need direction*
> *Direction and guidance*
> *And an open door.*
*And there it is*
*A door, partly obscured but open*
> *To what?*

*I'm encouraged, hopeful,*
> *And also waiting and waiting,*
> *And waiting*

■■■

When we returned to our Atlanta home, I discovered Nena Bryans in my college alumnae journal. She was featured as a former Christian educator turned sculptor. In the article she said, that when she worked in her studio while listening to classical music, "I'm as close to Heaven as you can get." I clearly knew what she meant. I contacted her in Pennsylvania. She had written a key book on art and faith, entitled *Full Circle: A Proposal to the Church for an Arts Ministry*. She sent me a copy which I immediately consumed.

She wrote how art impacts worship, the church's mission, social justice and education. Her words about the transforming power of art notably moved me. She cited Thomas Merton, how he "haunted" churches because of their art, and eventually found the Christ behind the art. She spoke of art as transforming power. Art as good news. Art kindling the spirits of those who felt long estranged from the church. I ruminated over her words and anecdotes.

Providentially we met some time later. Again, the encounter surprised me with someone "in the field of my bliss." She enrolled in a contemplative retreat for women in a monastery in Alabama which I facilitated for the Seminary. She came to Atlanta by train, and I drove us for four hours to the retreat center. For four hours we never stopped talking and sharing. How did you get interested in art? What led up to that? What did you do to develop your art? How have you done art in or with a church? Where are you now in your art making? What has helped you along the way? We both asked each other.

Since then, she and I have shared book titles, articles, and conferences that we needed to know about. She told me about the August 1995 conference on *Visual Arts and Religious Communities* held at the Pacific School of Religion in Berkeley. She urged me to join her in attending. So I journeyed back to California two years after my initial trip. In Berkeley, walking back and forth from my lodging to the conference the scent of eucalyptus trees enfolded me, the same scent I recalled that Mothers Day in Bolinas. It somehow confirmed my being at the conference.

About 400 people of different faiths and nationalities participated in the five-day conference. Widely known authors and lecturers from seminaries and universities led plenary sessions, usually accompanied with slides. Topics included discussions on the second of the Ten Commandments about: "no graven images," a prohibition against art or not? What is "sacred space?" Plus lectures on: contemporary film, Andean textiles, Indian art, icons, architecture and faith, on being an artist, spirituality in contemporary art, and interviews with painters.

In the rousing lectures:

Terrence said, "Art should illuminate, not illustrate; it should be polyvalent in meaning and therefore open the viewer to possibility."

Mary said, "Abstract art more clearly expresses the spiritual."

Cleve said, "Art, like prayer, is a hand stretching out into the darkness."

Thomas said, "With the Incarnation of Christ, we salute all matter with reverence."

Margaret said, "It's not the image itself that inspires, but the viewer's conceptual or emotional investment in it that makes the art inspire and evoke."

Tobi said, "We become what we gaze upon; therefore we must have good art around us all the time."

Diane said, "Art has power because it makes us *feel.*"

Cathy said, "The arts sensitize pastors and empower them to become more pastoral."

Jyoti said, "Art is a way to God." and "The mystic and the artist are the same."

And Seyed said "The artist's greatest work of art is the artist's own life."

I inhaled what I heard, deeply and ravenously.

Afternoon workshops addressed ethics and art, art in the community, art as outreach, the arts in worship and education, and visual poetry. Exhibitions of art, conversations with artists who showed their work in slides and albums, or who demonstrated the process of their work interspersed the lectures and workshops. The bookstore overflowed with exciting resources. It offered books galore on every kind of art, plus images on the walls and CD's of music. When I entered it I heard the ecstatic music of Hildegard of Bingen. I took the CD home with me. Her haunting chants empower me whenever I work in my studio.

The conference overflowed with stimulating people to talk to. I remember Joan, a Presbyterian associate pastor in Sausalito. We spoke of how to do art in the local church. "Go where they love you," she said. "Then when you fall on your face they will pick you up and encourage you forward." She had helped instigate a vacation Bible school in her church using art as the medium for teaching.

I remember Anne, who sat beside me in the plenary lectures, working on a quilt in her lap. She had pre-cut random shapes, and stitched them down by hand as she listened. It was a totally new form of quilt making for me. At the end of the conference she put the whole thing together on a library table and invited us to view it and to autograph it. I remember someone in the group gasping, "You don't turn under raw edges?" A woman, much older than I, responded, "Life's too short to turn under edges." That remark pointed to future directions for fabric projects of my own.

I remember encountering again Cathy Kapikian, a major presenter. She recognized me and expressed pleasure at seeing me in attendance. I was surprised that she had remembered me from the workshop I had done with her years before at my Seminary. Some time after that I had visited her at her Seminary, Wesley, in Washington, DC. She toured me around the campus, and I noted art work in every class room and in the stunning little Dadian Gallery. I noted the space for an on-going artist-in-residence. I hardly believed what I was seeing: how art, faith and theology were woven together. We had coffee together in the campus cafeteria. She encouraged me to keep exploring my artistic path. She recognized the grip that art was beginning to have on me. Again, here in Berkeley, she supported my artistic direction.

The words, thoughts, visual expressions and the vibrancy of the artists at the conference spun in my heart and mind. It would take months to absorb it all. I filled a notebook full of jottings. I tried to catalog as much as I could in my mind so the awesome insights and new information could be retrieved at a later time. All that I had heard and seen fed my emerging artistic self. The week in Berkeley began to confirm, *Yes, I am on the right path.*

## Paintings and a Container

I met up with Nancy again. True to her hospitable nature, she invited me to join her for a meal at a Mexican cafe. "So what has happened with you since we met two years ago?" she asked.

"I've been trying to find my way. I've been exploring different art forms — mainly painting."

I pulled out photos of five paintings I had done, plus one of the *Passion* quilt. I felt almost embarrassed over my beginner's attempts. I told her how the subject matter in the paintings had captured me and stirred deep feelings. How I loved painting with a palette knife. She commented on the textures the knife had created.

Then, she responded enthusiastically over my choice of colors in the *Passion* quilt. She asked how I went about making it, and I told her the story. Even in my beginning attempts, she recognized my urgency to make more art. Then she said, "I wish you had a container of sorts — a place, or ministry, or a position, even, — into which you could pour all your artistic efforts and gifts. To form a whole. To make *you* whole."

I wished for that, too. I had envisioned such a container. An arts ministry in a church — like Joan of Sausalito. A church or conference center where I could lead workshops on creativity and art making. A seminary or a college dedicated to combining art with faith where I could be artist-in-residence. To find such a container would be rare indeed. Plus I simply was not ready, with my five paintings and one quilt. At that point, I could only dream bold dreams.

Realistically speaking, however, such a container seemed far-fetched. It would take quite some time for me to be recognized and more importantly to recognize myself as an accomplished artist. I wondered if I had enough years of life left to realize this. Additionally I as a married woman and minister would have to weave my dreams in and out of commitments with a spouse, and around a family's and church's needs. Conflicting expectations impose improvisational attempts to create a whole — to "compose a life," as Mary Catherine Bateson has labeled such efforts. Priorities constantly shift with rising and falling demands. In spite of restraining circumstances, some women rise above them to create new identities for themselves. Others succumb to cultural expectations imposed on women of a particular era. As for me, with awkward attempts I wanted to compose my life around art making in the midst of domestic and ministerial concerns. It would mean re-inventing myself even as I negotiated responsibilities.

If I created a visual container to hold the concerns of my life, what would it include? Representations of ministry — perhaps a shepherd's crook, a cross, a Bible. And mothering: a child, a crib, a tricycle and even a Girl Scout pin, or a soccer ball. How to represent the closeness of marriage: rings? A wedding dress? But beyond that, what? Two taking coffee together? Holding hands? An embrace? And in it of course sat writing and art symbolized by a computer and a sewing machine.

During our lunch hour, Nancy saw and supported my desires. She wanted to know what my life looked like back home. I told her of my ministerial responsibilities. In Greater Atlanta Presbytery, I chaired a committee on hunger. I sat on a committee dealing with candidates for ministry. I helped launch another committee of spiritual formation and led monthly retreats for ministers. I visited members of a congregation on a regular basis. I was trying to write about my experiences in Africa, plus occasional devotionals for church publication.

In reciting to her my commitments and on-going engagements I realized that I painted a picture of a seriously fragmented life. In her presence I wondered where art lived among the shards of things to do. I admitted to stuffing art around the edges, in and among all the other activities. Clearly, it did not hold center attention. Would it ever?

She asked, "What would your life look like if you were in charge of it?"

The question took my breath away. I could not answer.

I seriously wondered if a woman immersed in a family is ever in charge of her life, as noted by Bateson. She would have to look at the givens and make allowances for them. Then, with fierce determination she would look at the remnants of her time and energy, pondering what she could do with the treasured leftovers. Perhaps if I could release all the non-family commitments which I had voluntarily and involuntarily taken on as a minister, then maybe I would be more or less "in charge." Maybe.

■■■

The photos of five paintings I had shown Nancy came from a series I called *The Light in the Forest*. The light falling on trees beyond my study window at home captured my attention. The sunlight illuminated some twigs and leaves, whereas others sank into darkness. With passing time, the light shifted. What was once in the dark became saturated with light, and vice versa. I gazed at the trees, transfixed by the play of light and the way the colors changed.

I was moved to write:

> *Sunlight sifting through trees*
> *Warming the darkness*
> *Setting aglow the golds and the greens*
> *Setting afire the reticent heart*
> *Kindling again the warmth of God's love.*

I also scrutinized light sifting through trees while on vacation with Pete in Tennessee. We stayed in a cabin by a creek surrounded by forest. He observed how, in the woods, I walked slowly, and absorbed everything around me. How I photographed a plant's leaves caught in sunlight, a water-covered stone shimmering like silver, sun's rays sliding down some tree trunks but not others. I was mesmerized.

My paintings responded to the shadows and lights of those wooded scenes. I did the first painting almost by accident. In cleaning up my acrylic paint, I wiped it on scrap paper with a palette knife. I loved the feel of applying paint this way. So, using the knife on a canvas board, I created the trunk of a dark pine tree highlighted by brilliant yellow light falling behind it. I smeared blues, yellows and creamy whites creating lesser lights farther behind the tree. Then with the point of the knife, I scraped into the paint to create foliage. I worked toward a luminosity in my choice of colors. I hoped viewers might experience the mystery and awe of light in the forest. I wanted to whet their appetite to seek out and explore their own forest glades.

Clearly, my efforts at painting matched my inner feelings, as had happened with the *Passion* quilt. *But did making art revolve around feelings alone? If this were so, would I be assured of what to do by how strongly I felt?* I rarely had passionate feelings when I engaged in writing. I did it more from a commitment to keep moving my fingers across my computer's keyboard to complete a project.

*So, where did this leave me?*

●●●

My encounters with the art world provoked deep questions and heartfelt yearnings. I remained unsure about what to do with these provocations. Determined to remain open, I learned what fed my soul. I learned what resources to absorb — books, conferences, exhibitions — and what artists were essential for me to meet. I learned I could not make art without suitable space to work in and that I needed the support of other artists around me. I gleaned enormous insights and information from the artists I met. Some encounters fell my way, others I boldly sought out. Personalities and artists supported my newfound interest: Nancy, Holly, Penelope, Nena, Cathy, even Belzelel, and attendees at the PSA Conference in Berkeley. I discovered painting and quilting techniques which excited me. The beauties and the colors of nature fed me. I recognized the sincere and warm affirmation my husband gave me.

All these colorful encounters and support directly and indirectly laid the groundwork for a growing vision for my artistic self. Days ahead would determine my niche in art making.

**THE LIGHT IN
THE FOREST**
12 x 15"
Acrylic on canvas

*"I was transfixed by the play of light
and the way the colors changed."*

# 3

# FINDING MY VOICE

❧

## A Turning Point

Dizzy from conversations and encounters in California, I returned to my home at a loss. I wanted to make art but what specific kind of art? I had the driving urge to communicate through shapes and colors. For me, my basic vision was to express joy and passion. I hoped to dazzle people with color. I hoped they would stand still and take a deep breath upon viewing my artwork. I hoped they would connect to liveliness and life, and beyond that, to God. How could I best express this?

The choice of a medium depended on what I wanted to say. Would painting express what I wanted to say? Or would fabric? I needed to find the physical medium that would transform my inner fervor into a concrete visual expression. My creative efforts longed to be released, not just imagined in my head. They had to move from my imagination out through my hands. Of course my ponderings inevitably ended with questioning: *who am I to say anything in an art form?* After all, I was a neophyte, an apprentice in art making, a beginner.

The logical, most accessible way for any of us to communicate is through words. Prior to the 1990's I aspired to be a writer. My world revolved around words. I soaked up books, jotting down captivating phrases and descriptions from fiction and non-fiction. I would stand in line at the bank or supermarket gazing at people, rolling novel lines around in my mind to describe them.

I wrote articles, devotionals and poetry primarily for church publications. I consumed books about how writers write. I even wrote a 300-page novel when I felt the world close around me with the advent of a third and surprising pregnancy.

When I entered theological seminary in mid-life, words dominated in writing, speaking and preaching. Everything in seminary and in ministry hung on words. Because I could write and speak well, I achieved a high academic standing, much to my satisfaction. Then I was ordained as a Presbyterian "Minister of Word and Sacrament." Of course "Word" refers to the Word of God which crowns all words. To be a minister of the Word refers to intense study of the Bible using others' scholarly work and incorporating knowledge of Greek and Hebrew in which the original texts were written. This arduous exercise results in the Sunday sermon. Thus, one reads, studies, preaches, hears and hopefully applies the Word to both minister and congregation. As a minister, I became a conduit for God's voice, through the Word by means of words. Words mattered — greatly.

In ministry, however, I soon realized that the preached word doesn't always reach its destination. Sermons often connect minimally with listeners. Different people hear different things. Tone of voice can change the meaning of words. Thoughts of listeners often roam to other topics, like plans for Sunday dinner. Further, words only point to how we understand God but never convey the whole truth or experience of God. They falter in their attempt to access the Holy.

I soon noticed that God uses many vehicles to communicate beyond words. Because God seems intent on not letting go of us, God finds ingenious ways to reach us. I found God communicating with me not only verbally but through silence, music and nature. How often I have sunk into a corner of my home lit a candle and touched God in the silence. As with Elijah in I Kings 19:12, I experienced God through "a still, small voice," or "the sound of sheer silence," as the phrase is variously translated.

In certain music, I could connect with God almost instantly as it lifted me beyond my preoccupations. I resonated with Taizé chants, Hildegard of Bingen's soaring chorales, Russian orthodox liturgy and the music of Navajo flute player, R. Carlos Nakai. Even though I rarely understood any of the words of the chants or choruses — the tunes held me in thrall. Words didn't matter.

Then with nature I often smiled with a sense of God's presence in the sun shining through red autumn leaves or moonlight rippling on a lake. Visually I had found God in the exuberance of design and color in nature. In each of these settings, my eye and ear brought my thinking and speaking to stillness. There in the depths of myself, in silence I peeled back traces of the Holy One.

Fay Key, a long-time spiritual friend, referred me to Psalm 19:1-4. Here the psalmist says that the heavens declare the glory of God. "There is no speech, nor are there words; their voice is not heard, yet their voice goes through all the earth and their words to the ends of the world."

"See?" she said. "Communication happens in many ways — even without words."

I stood on the precipice of discovering the presence of God in visual art.

■ ■ ■

My friend Connie and I visited an exhibit of collage artist Romare Bearden. He excelled at a number of media, but was known widely for his imaginative collages. I thought I had no interest in creating collages myself; still, I found his collage paintings extraordinary. As we wandered through the exhibit, I stopped over and over again to gaze at the outrageous noses and twisted eyes and mouths he had cut from magazines to create new faces. Clothing for his figures came from wallpaper, colored construction paper or more magazine pages. He sanded and bleached papers, plus added spurts of paint here and there. He set his characters in the midst of various activities: cooking, playing instruments or just lounging in a yard. Jazz musicians were a favorite theme. Many portrayed city life, or life in the tropics, the birthplace of his wife. A number of his subjects came from the Bible, such as Noah's ark and the return of the prodigal son. I viewed bizarre, flamboyant and exuberant images. His daring and originality startled me.

I found a quote of his tacked to the wall of the museum:

> The artist has to be something like a whale swimming around with its mouth open absorbing everything until he really has what he wants.

> When he finds that, he can start making limitations and then he really begins to grow.

His thought fit me like socks. Truly I was swimming around with my mouth wide open absorbing everything. Apparently it was absolutely OK to do so. His words gave me permission to keep on exploring. Perhaps all artists go through such an exploratory process. From what he said, hope rose within me. I would indeed find what I wanted. I would find a niche where my passion could incubate and grow. It would take time, but it would come.

I continued to try different art forms. In spite of having made one quilt and feeling a tug towards fabric art, I took classes at a local art center. I needed to discover what medium unequivocally called my name. I tried clay, and tapestry weaving. I delved into watercolor and acrylic painting: painting intuitively, painting still life, painting metaphysically, painting in nature, and painting from photographs. I attempted painting on silk. The night I swooped paint across a piece of tacked-down silk trying to image a flower, the teacher looked at me and said, "Oh, you must be an artist!" I gulped, "Well, I'm trying." What I really wanted to say to her was that I was swimming around like a fish with my mouth wide open.

On the days of my classes, I sprang into life as if reborn. The residue of paint under my fingernails identified me as a painter. With joy, I wore the paint like a badge.

Painting, however, raised more questions than answers for me. I encountered dozens of canvases and papers in various stages of creation, paintings in exhibits, homes and studios, plus painters themselves. I could not envision where any paintings of mine would fit into this vast sea of creativity. I could not see what kind of painting would reflect me and convey what I wanted to say. Again, what did I want to say?

■■■

In my explorations I did not give up on words. In pre-retirement, I thought I could do both writing and art. Articles published and unpublished languished in my files. Two book manuscripts percolated in my craw. I joined a writers group. But the writing soon became heavy and oppressive. I found no joy in it. Besides, if none of my reams of words saw the light of day in print — which was highly likely — then what was the point? I wondered why any of us struggling writers spend so many hours hoping to be published when the odds are totally stacked against us. I wrestled with the idea that my words would travel no farther than my computer. Isn't the time, effort, ink and paper usually wasted?

In an effort to infuse energy into my writing, I began a mandala journal of circular patterns. I bought a sketch pad and, drawing around a plate, I created circles on several pages at a time. Several mornings a week I picked up oil pastel colors, the ones which somehow spoke to me. I did not plan what to do — I just engaged the impulse of the moment. The patterns emerged out of sheer intuition and improvisation. I loved curving the colors this way and that. Perceiving the perimeter of the circle as my outer life, I viewed the core of the circle as my inmost being. Purples and reds appealed to me repeatedly. Instead of viewing them as anger or depression — two interpretations — they expressed my passion. I gave each mandala a title and a date.

For example, I recorded my struggle between art and writing with fierce serrated edges of orange half circles opposing each other within the larger circle. I called it "Torn Apart."

Later, I wrote: "Did the image represent two parts of myself needing to come together, or is there a creative tension in the abyss between the two halves which is far more valuable than I realize?" Then, upon returning to the congested city from the beautiful mountains, a mandala depicted my grief in a blue-black spiral which I called "Closed In."

Through these drawings I discovered that shapes, patterns and colors of visual images can be read. Whenever I opened the journal at a later date, I could remember my feelings as I looked back over the images. The events and circumstances on each date when I drew the mandala arose in my imagination. I could read the visual journal like a book, as if written in words, a significant discovery for me which would carry over into my quilt making.

In spite of wanting the art exercise to energize my writing the art making won out. Images, colors and designs captured me. I dreamed of them, pondered them and above all, was steeped in energy by them. I had unearthed the power of images. They reveal, teach and inform. They evoke possibilities. They can comfort and they can provoke longing. They can empower, transform and support.

Indeed, art can change the direction of a life, even mine.

■ ■ ■

With great perplexity, a friend asked me, "For heaven's sake, why don't you just dive head first into art? Just close the door to writing ... at least for awhile?

Me: "It's just not that easy."

Friend: "Why not?"

Me: "Because of feeling so responsible."

Friend: "Responsible for what?"

Me: "Responsible for my gift — my ability to write well."

Friend: "Whatever do you mean?"

Me: "I keep remembering what Flannery O'Connor said, 'A gift is a considerable responsibility'."

Friend: "Then you've put yourself on a guilt trip. Besides, suppose you have more than one gift?"

Me: "That's the trouble."

Friend: "What trouble?"

Me: "Trying to figure out which gift to pursue."

Friend: "Then go for the Joy. Life is too short!"

Me: "But people keep saying how my writing has helped them. How it's been meaningful. They ask what I am working on now. Shouldn't these comments say that I'm on the right track and I just need to get busy and produce?"

Friend: "You don't need to listen to them. Listen to your heart."

Me: "That's hard. Really hard."

I was too rational to listen to my heart. Too logical to consider what I felt.

Fortunately a different O'Connor intervened. She challenged my thoughts on responsibility. Elizabeth O'Connor said that our life's direction may change. Different ages and stages of life call forth different gifts. A new ministry may emerge with new gifts, circumstances and longings. For one gift to flourish, we must shut the door on others.

▪▪▪

I had set foot into the visual art world with my *Passion* quilt, but I kept being pulled into writing. *How was I going to juggle these two interests?* Realistically, I had no time to invest in both. What to do with writing? The answer surfaced dramatically in my writers group of four men and me. We met every three weeks to critique what each other had written. The experience so battered me that I lost confidence in myself as a writer. The gentle, wise leader and a published writer himself, intercepted our discussion and criticisms more than once. He believed in me and encouraged my gift.

I had been trying to write a memoir of our living for thirteen years in West Africa. The group bemoaned over and over that my writing failed to reveal my feelings. I tried one thing and then another. I believed that writing should show, and not tell. Apparently they wanted more telling through more feeling-freighted words. I re-worded sentences, tried different points of view, made sure that verbs carried the weight of the sentence and not adjectives and adverbs. I wrote and re-wrote to no avail. I could not understand why my feelings weren't obvious and they could not perceive why I couldn't produce what they suggested.

Finally, I brought *Doorways to Passion* to a meeting. When it came time for my work to be critiqued, the same evaluation emerged. "Where are your feelings?" In desperation I pulled out my quilt.

"Here!" I exclaimed. "Here are my feelings. *This* is where they are emerging!"

The oranges, fuchsias, reds, blacks and hot pinks spilled out in rich profusion. Their vibrancy flooded the table before us. My action rendered the group speechless.

It was a turning point. I finally named my struggle. I couldn't produce what they wanted because energy for writing had vanished. The quilt testified to an expression of feelings beyond words: something still new to me, something unknown to them.

At the end of this meeting I left the group. After all, having stepped through doorways to passion, I could no longer invest in words. Moreover, life was short and art gave me life. Something in me would die if I didn't do it. So I walked out of that era of writing and closed the door.

**Transformation**

In May, 1996, another door opened when I enrolled in a two-week quilting course at Penland School of Crafts in the mountains of North Carolina. "My body and soul burrows into this cozy nest, and I smile," I wrote in my journal shortly after my arrival at Penland. The silent, verdant panorama encircled me and contrasted sharply with the noisy city life of my home in Atlanta. The ring of mountains all around the school sang of invitation and delight. Llamas fed languidly in the grassy field at the hub of the circle, their coats burnished gold by rays from the setting sun. Behind me the School vibrated with energy: from the forges, the kilns, the looms, the dye baths, the photo labs. Open day and night, teeming with college students, adult seekers, and retirees, the studios churned out incessant energy. Their vigor held me captive.

When my friend Gretchen arrived, we climbed the creaking stairs to the top of the historic Loom House. There we unloaded our sewing machines, fabrics and supplies. We had brought an inordinate amount of stuff with us because no shop existed within twenty miles to buy what we might need. My fabrics included all sorts of African prints collected over the years. We each had a work table to ourselves, a wonderful gift of space.

Then we surveyed the room. We gasped at the quilts on the walls created by our teacher, Terri Hancock. Appliquéd figures and designs crowded each quilt, pushing and shoving, fighting and arguing with each other. Puzzling configurations and juxtapositions of objects, like potato mashers and morning glories, rattled the viewer's sensibilities. Sticks — an obsession with Y-shaped sticks — reverse-appliquéd into wild background colors. Unbelievable realistic faces embroidered into the quilts. We shook our heads in astonishment. We looked at each other, laughed and said, "What have we gotten ourselves into?"

As we talked before going to sleep, Gretchen told me about a conference she had attended with her daughter. She mentioned a line a speaker had quoted from the Song of Songs: "My beloved...stands behind our wall; he looks through the window, showing himself through the lattice." Somehow the image of lattice captured me. I clung to it as I entered the classroom the next morning, my mind and imagination otherwise blank as copy paper.

About a dozen women sat at the work tables. Ranging in ages from 18 to 83, we varied in quilting experience. Yet enthusiasm floated up from each one and blended with the inviting fabrics, books and dynamic quilts Terri had brought with her. She offered teaching, suggestions and affirmations. But at rock bottom, the quilts we were to create would arise solely from no one but ourselves. From me. The *Passion* quilt had been someone else's idea. The log cabin strips in it came from an age-old formula. But now, I alone had to come up with a fresh design. But what and how?

I wanted to depict the transformation that had revitalized me while living in Ghana and Nigeria, West Africa. There, the poverty, lack of both conveniences and significant service opportunities, plus the relentless heat oppressed me and slowed my pace. I kept asking, "What am I doing here?" I had felt useless and unproductive. As a westerner, I was used to busyness, going out and about, and doing meaningful things. In the emptiness of both my spirit and the environment, God's Spirit intervened in my life. Only then did I view African hospitality, exuberance and beauty with a changed perspective and a changed me.

I puzzled how to express this invisible wonder from the past: how to translate feelings, experiences, insights into fabric art. I had to go slowly, take one step at a time, remain open to all possibilities and reject none in this embryonic stage. I sketched a few ideas. Nothing jelled. I had brought a cherished piece of shimmering blue and green tie-dyed twill from Ghana. I had never wanted to cut the highly prized fabric. Now I would use it as the background piece for my quilt. I stretched it out on the table, still uncertain what to do. I ran my fingers over the invigorating colors. *I will preserve this piece forever in my quilt*, I mused with pleasure.

The image of the lattice kept floating through my consciousness. On the second day, I started hand stitching tiny squares together into a cloth lattice. Uncertainty about the future use of the lattice did not deter me. It would reveal itself as I proceeded. The squares came from assorted prints in bright colors of orange, purple, reds, greens, and blues from my stash and from sister quilters. The lattice, with square and rectangular openings cut into it, revealed the blue-green tie-dyed piece. The openings acted as windows to allow the tie-dyed fabric underneath to shine through. I envisioned the lattice attached to the top of the quilt which would hang freely over the blue-green background.

It took me a week, working about ten hours a day, to finish the lattice. Unlike the silent weaving room on the floor below us — where weavers warped their looms and counted stitches with great concentration — our room rang with boisterous laughter and talking. People from all over the campus heard us and trooped up the stairs to join the fun. It all rolled over me. I sat at my table in the back of the room and focused on my stitching, oblivious to the noise around me. I discovered a quietness enfolding me like a cloak. I stitched in peace, totally absorbed in my work amidst all the bustle, and the rise and fall of sound around me.

In attaching the lattice overlay to the top of the tie-dyed background, I realized it told my story. The colorful little pieces jammed together represented my bubbly, busy life in the United States. I equated the blue-green tie-dye background with God's Spirit increasingly peeking through the openings in the lattice and gradually becoming evident in the chaos of my life. At the bottom of the overlay, I hung a Ghanaian symbol from yellow ribbons. The symbol, *gye nyame* ("except God") from African traditional religion, adorns many Christian worship spaces. It represents the omnipotence of God with the saying, *No one knows the beginning or the ending of creation except God.*

During the second week, I worked on the bottom of the quilt. I incorporated leaves outlined in navy batik from a neighbor's discarded dress worn in Ghana. More symbols peeped out among the leaves — symbols of wisdom, endurance and love. I sewed down beads, a new experience for me: bugle beads, seed beads, sequins, plus small African cowrie shells. The overall design signified the fertile spiritual growth that had enlivened me during those years.

Nothing could be more enchanting than playing with these colors and patterns. Nothing could be more delightful than to watch the design of the quilt unfold right under my fingertips each day. No other medium had mesmerized me so profoundly. I never felt more alive, more centered, more in my element. *This* is what I need to do. *This* is where my heart dwells. Making art out of fabric truly is my bliss.

*I had found my voice, I discovered my artistic niche.*

Amazement over the whole process gripped me. Thankfulness flooded me from toes to hairline. I had not wasted hours wondering what to create, seeking a design or inspiration. Everything had come gratuitously to me and at the right time. Indeed, the surrounding props served as lamps along a dark path: other students and their work, quilt books and conversations with Gretchen. Our teacher's wild imagination sparked my own and made me realize that absolutely anything can go into a quilt! In combination, they illuminated a way forward with my fabric and design. But at rock bottom, I birthed the quilt, something rather unbelievable to me. I wrote in my journal: *I can't get over the quilt I've created...how it came out of nowhere and how unique it is...I've never seen anything like it in any of the quilt books here, and there are plenty of them!* Of course, the quilt had not blossomed out of nowhere. It arose from my intuition and imagination, long asleep but now fully awake. Vitality, passion and voice sparked my inner being. I knew I had to trust this new fiery energy, and go where it pointed. It had taken me by the hand and led me into a new territory.

I discovered courage linked with the new energy. When one works improvisationally, when one doesn't know how to begin or where to go, the backbone of courage is needed. Courage and audacity arise from the burning desire to create. Here I had the tools, the resources, the creative atmosphere of Penland, the uninterrupted time and the vibrant fabrics pulling me to make something with my hands. The insistent urge had over-ridden any timidity and hesitation on my part. It made *what-if's* and *maybe's* melt away.

In the creative realm, courage enables that first cut into fabric or first stroke of paint or first touch of the clay without worrying about messing up or wasting time, money or supplies. It can push one off familiar maps to create a potter's shed in the backyard, or a room in the home for a studio. Courage kindled a transformation in me, not only in finding my voice in making my first art quilt, not only in a divine revitalization while living overseas, but in my venturing forth into the world of visual art.

I named the quilt *Transformation: An African Journey.*

I finished the quilt at home within two months with more beading, quilting and then binding. I quilted it with heavy six-strand embroidery floss to emphasize the stitching. I had to stab the fabric with a robust needle and pull it through to the other side with needle-nose pliers. I wondered if this way of quilting would pass muster among quilters. Then I laughed. The fundamental lesson the course taught me stared me in the face: there are absolutely no rules for art quilts. I can do anything on and with fabric. Again, as I discovered in my first quilt, a sense of freedom took hold within me. This realization made me float high on the wings of adventure and untried possibilities. I needed no permission to engage fully in this art form. I could make fabric creations wherever my imagination, resources and work would take me.

An invitation came my way to exhibit the *Transformation* quilt. Author Sue Monk Kidd was to speak in Atlanta. Seminar leaders invited participants to bring art objects to decorate the space. I hesitated and wondered if I dared bring my quilt. So I asked one of the leaders of the event. She looked at my work, and said "Go for it!"

On the night of the seminar, I nervously entered the meeting space, quilt in hand. It was the first time to show any work publicly. My initial boldness turned into astonishment. *Who do you think you are to do this?* I asked myself. Surprisingly my identity seemed to merge with the quilt. It was I, and I was it. I felt like a plowed field, raw, laid wide open for anyone to trample on. *Why should anyone view my work? What have I to offer in this space among these creative people? What was I trying to prove, or at best, to say?* Questions swarmed in my head.

Summoning up courage, I resolutely followed through and hung my quilt. Then, many things to say swept over me like a gale. Chiefly my work spoke of God's ability to change people. After all the name of the quilt declared that fact. It said that people can grow and become more deeply rooted spiritually. That Africa spawned such growth for me after I was plucked from the frenetic atmosphere of America. My life had been renewed. My quilt testified that out of Africa beautiful surprises emerged.

At the event, Sister Loretta exclaimed over the work. My friend Mary nodded enthusiastic approval. My friend Betty said "Wow!" My anxieties slowly melted. I felt a sense of empowerment that I had truly found my voice, and it was speaking clearly and boldly.

Previously, I had pondered how wordless art could communicate anything about the Good News of God's love. I had discovered God's speaking through nature, in silence and in music. Now I learned that visual art, even my art, had the capacity to speak.

■■■

I had read Sue's book, *The Dance of the Dissident Daughter* prior to her lecture. Her words on creativity had gripped me:

> Ask yourself: 'What is my deepest passion, *really?* What moves me profoundly?' Let the answer float up from the truest, most vulnerable place in your heart. Greet this answer like it is your own newborn self being placed in your arms. Love it. Bond with it, feed it.... We need to commit to our creative path ... and actually do it.... Being committed means learning what we need to know and doing what we need to do to make the voice of our soul heard.

"Yes, yes, yes!" I wrote in the margins of the book. I celebrated my passion. I had found my voice. Now I needed to commit seriously, intentionally to my artistic path. With determination I needed to make time to do my art. I needed to exploit experiences that would enhance my creativity and develop my skills.

The vacated third bedroom of our apartment became my studio. Later, for a period of time a storage room in the guest house where we lived opened up with large windows and empty walls. There, I set up my machine, a large table, most of my fabric and a big design wall. Away from phone and other distractions the space allowed me to work in bliss. I began to develop a box of file folders with articles about artists, exhibitions, and notes about art retreats and workshops.

I enrolled in workshops on creativity, design and quilt-making, locally and out of state. I learned from Larkin van Horn at Grunewald Guild in Washington state, and Natasha Kempers-Cullen at Arrowmont School of Arts and Crafts. I sought out artists and quilters. I collected books and subscribed to magazines on art quilts. I visited every exhibition involving fabric that I noticed in the Atlanta newspapers, at the Connell Gallery, and in art centers at Callanwolde and Spruill. I viewed art in all forms to keep alive my visual acuity: exhibits of Nigerian art, Henry Ossawa Tanner, John Twachtman and the Five Rings exhibit at the High Museum during Atlanta's Olympics, pottery of Judith Duff and John Dotson, jewelry of Virginia Gailey all in Brevard, NC, and fiber arts exhibits, tapestry weaving and decorative gourd art in north Georgia. In New Mexico I savored Georgia O'Keeffe's and Ansel Adams' work, in St. Louis I took in the Museum of Contemporary Religious Art, and in Washington DC the Textile Museum and the gallery of the National Cathedral in Washington DC, an exhibit featuring *Faith in Fabric*. Getting as close to exhibits as I could, I soaked up patterns of design, layers of colors, the resourcefulness of mixed media, skills in stitching and weaving, and the applications of paint. I scribbled notes, I made sketches, and where possible, I took photos of the wonderful, diverse world of artists' work. I was learning and absorbing on my own.

I was becoming self-taught.

**TRANSFORMATION: AN AFRICAN JOURNEY**
27.5" x 37"

*"Learning that anything can go into a quilt I found a design with my fabic."*

# 4

## QUESTIONING MY PATH

### The Artist, The Writer, The Minister

Although I had found my voice in quilt making, I continued to have a commitment also to ministry. As a minister in pre-retirement years, I could not barricade myself in a studio, disengaged from people. I had to be involved with members of my congregation and persons in the wider community. My ministerial functions revolved around both doing and being, a ministry of action and presence. Sitting at bedsides of the sick, offering prayer for the bereaved, chairing committees, teaching classes, overseeing the church plant, and leading worship with preaching.

I had seen from my visit with Nancy Chinn that art also can be ministry. God's call to Bezalel had moved me deeply. But how would art fit into my call as a minister? If I were both minister and artist, time would be taken away from sermon preparation, visiting, and administration. With the diminishment of normal ministerial functions on my part, would the church authorities who ordained me and who yearly validated my call have second thoughts about my serving as a minister? Could the church view art as a call from God? That would be new to them. Minister-writers abounded but not minister-artists. None of us could point to a minister that we knew and say, yes, she or he is also called to engage in art as a legitimate part of ordained ministry.

Validation of a call by others, both lay and clergy, is essential among Presbyterians. I and other discerning members in the congregation and in the broader church have to agree that a certain path is God's path for the individual minister. In this chapter, I relate in depth my quandaries over a call into art because of the issue of validation and wanting reassurance that I was hearing God's call clearly. In no way did I want to jeopardize my call to ministry. If that would happen, I might have to abandon art altogether. I longed to find a minister who was also an artist. I would have asked him or her: *How did you discern your call? How do you integrate art with ministry? What was the process you went through to have church authorities validate your ministry?* Without such a person I was on my own, similar to my trying to complete my first quilt without my instructor's advice and encouragement.

The various roles, aspirations and gifts confronted me head-on at a retreat I attended. I wasn't prepared for what unfolded. The leader assigned a scripture passage for meditation from Mark 5:1-20 — the story of Jesus and the Geresene mad man. He named himself Legion, because he said he had multiple unclean spirits in him. I immediately connected. After reflecting on the story, I wrote in my journal:

> *My name is Legion. I call myself this because there are several persons living inside my skin. Too often these inner persons strive against one another. We tear at and yell at each other, and push and shove one another until one lands on top and is in charge. But only for a small increment of time because the others get restless and want to have their say and their day, and, it's a fight all over again.*

I saw that my Legion is inhabited by the artist, the writer and the minister, all in conflict. The artist demands her turn, waving around colorful fabric pieces or paint brushes. But the minister and the writer try to subdue her, calling her a young whipper-snapper with no track record. The writer claims to have the most credibility, and therefore wants to assume leadership. But the minister points out that she is the only one with a legitimized sense of call and function, recognized officially by the church. "If it weren't for me, you, artist, and you, writer, would stay isolated in an ivory tower!"

The *writer* argues that ministers can very well proclaim God's love through writing — more than any *artist* can, and *she* should take control. The *artist* points out that the *writer* is tired and worn out and can hardly churn out a page a week. "Whereas for myself," she says, "I'm bursting with enthusiasm and energy. So it's my turn."

They argue, and shout and shove until they see someone coming up the hill, someone who may be able to halt the ongoing struggle. For he is the Lord, Creator and Enabler for each of them.

In my imagination, Jesus tells them to recall the words of I Corinthians 12, speaking of gifts in the life of the church. No one in the church, as the body of Christ, can say "You don't belong" or "I don't belong to the body." Speaking to the three persons, he seems to say "You are all part of Martha Jane's body and life, but I am the head. You each have a function — sometimes parallel to each other, sometimes alternating. You need to stop competing and trying to take over by pushing and shoving. You don't need to evaluate or criticize. None of you is in charge. Only I am." Jesus also advised, "Simply take turns as children on a playground. When your turn comes, seize the day. Further, try to relax and enjoy the ride!"

I sat dazed at what had emerged. *Take turns.* I recalled hearing this as a child and then applying it to my own children. It made enormous sense now.

I investigated several models through books and people. When I asked Tunde, gifted Nigerian artist, musician and storyteller, how he managed his three-ring circus, he said it was according to commissions he had received. Well, I had no commissions, but I knew that circumstances, invitations, and engagements would doubtless dictate which gift to focus on and when.

I read that author Agnes Sanford, gifted with writing, a healing ministry, painting and drama, took different weeks of the year to focus on one gift at a time.

M.C. Richards resisted cultural expectations to excel in just one field. She kept pottery, poetry and teaching alive in her life. She finally realized that being dispersed was okay. She finally "hit upon an image: a seed sower. Not to worry about which seeds sprout. But to give them as my gift in good faith."


## Passion and Gifts

God has endowed each follower with gifts, graces and abilities for the good of others. They are nothing to brag about, just as beautiful eyes are nothing to brag about. They are just given. We have no control over their appearance in our lives. Thank God for the huge variety of gifts bestowed on everyone, because where I am lacking in ability or perception, you will fill in the deficit. Boredom would set in if everyone were alike, if everyone possessed the same abilities. Sufferings of the human race would mount up without the help, energies, and passions of others expressed through their gifts.

Some people wrongly say they have no gift, or they have never discovered any. Some of us have shone with our one gift throughout our lives, offering it in the context of the world's needs. Others juggle two or more gifts by integrating them into their life of service, or else taking turns to use one and then another as Jesus suggested in my imaginary scene. Our gifts lead us in various ventures and directions.

Paralysis may creep into my bones as I try to sort out which direction to go, and how to use which gift with my time and energy. Someone once exclaimed that it was "marvelous" I was so gifted. I responded that several gifts can be a burden. An assortment of too many options often stymies me, I explained. It's difficult to know which gift to honor on a given day. "Which end of the house to go to this morning? My study or my studio?" graphically describes my dilemma.

Is there ever a day presented to us like a blank canvas and we have the pleasure of asking "What might I do today?" not always, "What *must* I do today?"

We wake up with agendas, a list in our heads as we climb out of bed. We may like to engage in some creative project. Something that fires our bones. But alongside our wants there are needs. We most likely tend to the needs first. We try to clear the deck of responsibilities before we get down to what we would like to do. Yet, in the midst of busy necessities various perceptions, abilities or skills are pulled out of us, sometimes under great stress. Sometimes with great surprise. Too often we think we cannot handle an overwhelming challenge, but with surprise, we find we can reach deep down within ourselves and draw on resources of rich past experiences from our personal history. We find the emergence of unexpected gifts in the midst of crises, like the ability to tend to a critically ill person or the ability to calm fearful people. These unexpected gifts arise from our innate creativity. Just because they cannot be classified as *art* or *craft* does not negate the fact that they are expressions of our creative selves. Art and craft spill over into everyday challenges for there is an art in overcoming a financial crunch at home or in business, an art to placating a customer who pitches tantrums in an office, an art in making a marriage work.

Our energy to employ a gift may fluctuate. We may experience passion to tap into one gift and then it shifts the next day. Passion may skip to another interest or vanish altogether, for awhile or longer. With such a hop-scotch approach we wonder if anything can be accomplished although we intuitively know that passion must fuel any project, program or aspiration if we want to bring it to life. So we stay tuned for passion whenever it surges into our lives, or merely beckons shyly at the door.

■ ■ ■

I struggled to find my own rhythm of integrating the gifts of art and writing into my life around the edges of my ministry. They need not fight each other, as Jesus had reassured. So I tried taking turns by compartmentalizing my life by the week rather than by the year as Agnes had done. I thought I could write during most mornings and do art over the weekend or in the afternoons. A small art project could be completed in a short time frame, or I could engage in a long term project whenever time allowed, without pressure for completion without an end result in mind.

The plan folded. Saturdays and afternoons generally drowned in appointments or domestic chores, and Sundays were devoted to ministry. Too many last minute happenings created havoc with my week's planning. Ministry, art, and writing interlaced with providing food, clothing and presence for my family. Church members' needs interrupted my schedule almost every week. My time became fractured. One commitment took charge and then another. Art making would too easily fall to the bottom of priorities. In many situations, making quilts or painting did not seem as critical as getting supper on the table, or visiting a dying parishioner in the hospital. As I plunged into one engagement, mined one creative effort, honored one commitment at the expense of others, I told the neglected ones, Calm down. Your turn will come. I also told myself to loosen up. Try sowing seeds. Trust God that some will sprout.

■ ■ ■

Moments of enlightenment peppered my inner landscape. People, events, readings crossed my path just at the right time to give direction.

One occurred when I was stuck in traffic on Briarcliff Road in Atlanta. I was pondering an insidious guilt over squirreling myself away to make art. But there amid a go-slow line of cars I suddenly glimpsed the needed pattern. Becoming isolated to do art and then sharing it parallels the same process the minister undertakes in sermon preparation and delivery. She disengages from everyone, enters a space to craft the sermon entirely alone, and then goes out to grace the community with her creations. Retreat, solitude, sharing — essential in the creative process, whether making a sermon or a quilt. *Yes!*

Then, upon reading *The Quiet Eye: A Way of Looking at Pictures* by Sylvia Judson, a quote leaped out to me and burned itself into my remembrance. She said, "The artist serves humanity by feeding its hungry spirit in as real a sense as if he fed its hungry bodies." *Yes!* Art feeds the hungry spirit!  Certainly as a minister I had encountered hungry spirits: people under stress, people lacking vision, people on a treadmill of the same-old-same-old, people searching for meaning. In my own life I had discovered the healing power of images, the vitality of color. The relief of pain and stress came through my art making. Through non-verbal means I had accessed the Holy who transformed me through art. Might this also happen to others?

## God's Will, God's Longing

As I began to create quilts, I longed to fully engage in art. I also longed for certainty in direction and received only sporadic pointers, with darkness lying like a fog over me. Finally, finally I began to realize that none of us can make wise choices with absolute clarity. A sense of direction is encompassed in mystery and ambiguity. Being creatures with limitations, we can never know for sure which path to take. God gives us illumination only one step at a time. We are given light for only one day or one moment. Referring to a need for direction, someone has said, "You take a step. You pay attention. You decide which way to go for the next step."  It is well to ask ourselves what is the one very next thing we need to do? We don't need to see the whole forest necessarily — just one tree at a time, and trust God for the rest of the landscape.

A prayer by Thomas Merton spoke deeply to me because his truthful doubting struck a chord. He knew he could not make clear decisions. I resonated with his opening words, "My Lord God, I have no idea where I am going. I do not see the road ahead." Merton recognizes honestly that though he may think he is following God's will he may not in fact be doing so. Yes, yes, I agreed. "But I believe that the desire to please you does in fact please you." This desire, he believes, will lead him "by the right road." He declares his trust in God's direction for his life even when "lost or in the shadow of death" and affirms that God is always with him so he will not face his perils alone.

Indeed, I knew that desire could be tricky. The desire to please God, the desire to do art: I could see how they might be at odds. Do I have to pit one against the other? Certainly God must have put in me this desire, this passion to make art at the outset. God has given me this gift of art making to be used and to please God with it. Not to question it forever. My improvisational art with its spurts of passionate energy to guide the way has led me into God's will.

"God's will." Much verbiage has flooded books, tracts, essays and devotionals on how to find God's will for your life and mine. As Christians, we strongly desire to follow God's will because we believe that in God's will we will find fulfillment, usefulness and happiness. But we find it exasperatingly difficult to discern what that will is because our own wishes and agendas intrude. We have tools, however, at our disposal. Prayer, plus paying attention to circumstances, mental notations and feelings help point the way. Still, too often my *oughts* and my *wants* impose themselves on my sense of God's will. I ask myself repeatedly, *is it God's voice I am hearing or my own?* I used to think that the difficult, odious thing to choose constitutes God's will. It has to be hard to do. It has to consist of self-sacrifice. I've heard people say that they don't want to know God's will because they think "God will make me go to deepest, darkest Africa," apparently the epitome of self-oblation. Certainly with me, the oughts of ministry and the oughts of writing sat heavy on my shoulders in discerning the *wants* of a path into art.

At this juncture I encountered another perspective: how about God's will as God's delight? Eric Liddell, the famed Olympic runner, said he liked to run because "it gives God pleasure." I had never before considered giving God pleasure or delighting God. But I somehow began to sense that God delights in seeing us joyfully fulfilled in using our God-given gifts. A circular pattern of receiving and giving thrives between God and ourselves. God gives, I receive, and with pleasure, I offer back to God the fruition of my gifts, delighting God and others in the process. This circle of give and take extends our ministry surprisingly to God. In a nutshell, we are God's. Our gifts are God's. All that I am and have and do belong to God. So when I use any of my gifts, I am giving them back to God. In the words of the hymn: "We give thee but thine own, what-e'er the gift may be: All that we have is thine alone, a trust, O Lord from thee."

Following this thought, suppose I view God's will as God's longing for me? "What is the piece of God's dream that God has entrusted to me?" I read in a brochure of spiritual guidance programs. Discerning this piece I'd then ask: how would I function out of this dream? If engaging in art is God's will and God's longing for me, I wondered where my care for the rest of the world would fit in. Howard Thurman claimed that we need not ask this question. Rather, "Ask what makes you come alive and do that, for what the world needs is people who have come alive." A new aliveness had certainly enveloped me. But did vitality and passion comprise the only keys to unlock and open the door to my vocation as an artist? My questions and Thurman's words haunted me, licked my heels, and rumbled in the night.

## Questions

I recall several startling questions which loomed before me, giving incisive direction. They dealt with one's mortality.

Years before, I had attended a start-up conference for newly ordained ministers in order to set goals in ministry. One exercise posed the stark question: "How would you write your obituary? How would you respond to: 'She was known as _____'." The question jolted me, especially since the conference focused on beginnings, not endings. After catching my breath, I wrote in the line "minister and author of spiritually provocative books," which was my goal at the time. Filling in that blank brought to the surface my unspoken, unrecognized desire. I could no longer hide behind vague dreams. I had named *writing* as an insistent part of me that needed attention and commitment, not just vain wishing. Now, after shutting the door on writing, I would have to name my more recent goal: minister and fabric artist.

Later I discovered a similar question developed by Ignatius of Loyola, spiritual guide of the sixteenth century. He asked those who sought direction to imagine themselves on their deathbed. "What would you be grieved over for not having done in your life?" Asked of me, I instantly knew the answer:

"Making art." This was followed by a similar question that my friend Connie asked me one day: "What would you do if you knew you had only a year to live?" With no hesitation, I responded, "Do art."

I carried these three questions, one following on the heels of the other, around with me for weeks. They jammed a seeming backpack I never laid aside. I always had been a question asker, sometimes out of curiosity, most often out of insecurity, such as: *Am I on the right path, doing the right thing?* In my sixties it became crucial for me to know that I had taken the right path. Probing my identity and role in this new climate of creativity pointed me to the full realization about the frailty and unpredictability of the days ahead of me. Life is short. *I* am mortal. I *am* mortal. I am *mortal.* And time rushes down the raceway to eternity.

Still, I must do what I can until the sun goes down. Yes, art has sprouted in my life with insistent urgency. But, yes, I am also a writer, a minister, a family member. I'm not willing to relinquish any one of these roles. I needed to take turns with them all. One friend commented rather outlandishly that I needed to live four lives in order to do all that I felt called to do!

I have viewed the choices and attractions in my life as a cafeteria and filled up my plate until it overflowed. (This was especially true after my desert-like life in Africa where few opportunities for service or for artistic involvements presented themselves.) I can't seem to narrow down options. I have wanted everything! A little of this, a little of that, and oh my, doesn't that hold an attraction? Shouldn't I give this other possibility some attention?

I felt like the old woman who lived in a shoe who had so many children she didn't know what to do, so she gave them some broth without any bread, and whipped them all soundly and put them to bed. Of course the children would wither away and die if she did this. I saw giving a few children at a time my attention. I won't kill the others from neglect, but again, take turns. The old woman seemed to be advising me to view my gifts as living organisms: *Put some to bed. Don't put them out of your life.* Again, *take turns.*

I still have trouble sorting out the important things to do. I was, and still am, plagued with too many children/possibilities yammering for attention. Ideas for creative projects along with burning necessities daily crowded my mind then and do so now. Never mind that I wake up at night or go grocery shopping or pump gas, and some compelling idea for a quilt floods over me. Never mind that dozens of images and ideas filled and continue to fill notebooks (and even my prayer time), and my closet now overflows with unused fabrics, and my file drawers brim with partial or completed manuscripts, and ideas for writing saunter through my mind at unpredictable interludes.

Never mind that, even retired, I wear the hat of a minister, who preaches, teaches and visits occasionally. Workshops and retreats intersperse my days along with artistic functions. My family is woven into all this: my husband, and two faraway sons and a daughter along with five grandchildren.

Feeling like a juggler I seize one day at a time and consciously seek direction about this one twenty-four hour jewel. With gratitude, I open the gift that each day presents. Every morning begins in sublime peacefulness in our mountain home. I try to carry it with me all the day long.

## Feelings

Ignatius also discussed at length *consolations* and *desolations*. He said that we cannot make decisions with our minds alone. Feelings must play a vital part. For instance, when faced with a decision, if I experience joy, energy and excitement over a possibility, that is *consolation* — the notion of coming alive as in the Thurman quote. *Desolation*, on the other hand, brings feelings of heaviness, oppression, and darkness. To make a decision during desolation would be life-draining rather than life-giving. Looking at consolations and desolations in decision-making helps one to avoid a poor choice. The idea of examining my feelings over a choice seemed new to me. I had usually resorted to making lists of pros and cons, using my mind only. Soon a chance for me to experience the feelings of consolation and desolation came unequivocally.

It became a benchmark in future discernment predicaments.

One afternoon, I came into our kitchen after participating in a graveside service in Georgia July heat. Lathered in sweat, I listened to my answering machine. The dean of my college invited me to apply for the position of chaplain. I couldn't believe it. For several months previously, I had been thinking how I would relish being a college chaplain with its opportunities to engage in creative worship. Certainly this unexpected invitation merging with my excitement over the prospect pointed propitiously toward a direction designed by God. I was dead wrong.

The application process involved a grueling all-day visit on the campus. I interviewed with the president, the vice president for development, deans and then with a group of students. By the end of the day, I saw many aspects of college chaplaincy that I had not considered. I felt totally out of sync with the issues of young college women. Creative worship services comprised only a tiny part of the total job description. I realized that I had no energy for the position, no sense of joy in contemplating it. A pervasive heaviness engulfed me. For two weeks I dangled until the college finally called someone else. I felt a tremendous relief.

A month later I asked a friend who had a robust spiritual direction practice, "What was this experience all about?"

He quickly responded, "To teach you about consolation and desolation. Now you know how the two feel."

Ignatius' idea of consolation gave me grand permission to fully develop my art — if I would only listen to my feelings instead of constantly overriding them with my mind.

I had experienced desolations and consolations in other major decisions in my life but knew nothing about those concepts and how they could help in decision-making. At the end of two years of college, for example, I felt led by God to enter nursing school. I applied only in early August, figuring that God's will would be revealed to me if God opened the door at that late date. I would be expected to follow. Almost miraculously, I was accepted into the program which would begin in September. But I balked. I became fearful. My excitement about the prospect totally bottomed out. I didn't really want to leave my college. I was experiencing desolation without knowing how to interpret it. My wise minister urged me to stay in college and God would continue to call me into nursing if that was God's plan. So, after receiving my BA degree I entered nursing school, confident and with joy.

In reviewing the above experiences of desolation, I see now I put great stock in circumstances, in the doors that opened favorably and unexpectedly. But they cannot be the only indicators in decision-making. I also understood how feelings cannot become smothered under mental ruminations. The decision to marry Pete, the decision to move overseas as missionaries and my decision to enter seminary came not only from cognitive considerations, research, and talking with others, but going with my heart's desire. Perhaps it took a certain amount of growing up to allow feelings to enter the decision-making process. Why is it we distrust them? Or distrust intuition? Of course some personality types make decisions based solely on feelings, and others, like myself in my youth, exclude feelings and just mentally ponder the path to take.

●●●

In my search for direction, I scoured books about discernment. One book stood out above others with its concrete exercises and ideas, *Listening Hearts: Discerning Call in Community*. In order to discern vocation, more than thirty questions are posed by a group to a person seeking guidance. Quaker in origin, the group is called the Clearness Committee, called together to help a person to discern the answer to a problem. The questions usually asked by the Committee and recorded in the book enabled me to probe the hidden depths of my longings. Since the questions came from a source beyond me, not out of my inner need, they helped me be more detached. I recorded the following answers to a few of the questions:

*Do you have an image or vision of your potential ministry?*

I see a "giving birth to" a form of proclamation and the feeding of souls through art.

*What are the benefits of your course of action?*

To enable others to see/experience/feel God in new ways. To nurture the fires of the soul.

*What are its risks or hazards?*

That my efforts will never get exposure, that I will fall flat in my efforts, that pride will take over when I do succeed.

*Is this course you are considering motivated by zeal or by love?*

My zeal to share new approaches to God, and my love for a dying, unimaginative and unaware church and culture.

*What are your feelings? How intense are they?*

I have intensely passionate feelings about art as a means to communicate the Gospel.

There it is: feelings definitely enter the quandary about following a call into art.

Only in 2012 have I begun to realize the primary source of my hesitation to accept art into my life and to call myself an artist. It has to do with the process I went through to become an ordained minister. In the Presbyterian church, for a person to become a minister others in the church have to recognize that call. The person cannot simply get up and declare, "I've been called by God and I am going to become a minister and take a church." Indeed, a call by God to an individual has to occur. But governing bodies in the church also must recognize that call along with the giftedness of the individual to take on the role of minister. The governing body of the church — the Session — must recognize the call, then the Presbytery and a seminary in multiple committees and meetings with the individual. This means the individual seeking to become ordained is affirmed on that path on many levels.

I had no such affirmation in contemplating a call into art. Who was to say I had such a call and gifts to become an artist? Such affirmation of course is tricky. Hearing viewers rave over one's art work may be an ego trip, or truly constitute an affirmation of a call. Needless to say, in the beginning I had no body of work to be examined by anyone. I recall one such affirmation in November 2002. My neighbor and friend Roberta Martin and I went on retreat in a desert setting outside Tucson, AZ called Picture Rocks Retreat Center.

During one of the days we were instructed to contemplate in silence the question, "Who am I?" Prolific questions rolled over me. *Is my art a cop-out or an escape from the sufferings around me? How am I serving the world or trying to change the world or feeding hungry spirits through my art? Is any of this realistic? Is my artistic passion a gift, or an attachment?* I clearly felt oppressed, a pillar-to-post, mixed up person. When I relayed some of this to Roberta, she looked at me fully in the eye and said, "There is no question that you have the gifts and the call."

I escaped to the Center's chapel to mull over her words. There on the walls, emblazoned by sunlight shimmered the words: *The desert will lead you to your heart and there I will speak.* I asked myself, *What is in your heart to do?* Early on with the *Passion* quilt, I began listening to my heart. I resolved to keep listening, recognizing Ignatius' idea to include feelings in decision-making.

## A Quilt Symbolizes How Direction Happens

Recognizing the significance of consolations and desolations I let them guide me in making the next quilt. Because I had no sense of direction when I started the next quilt, I paid close attention to the waxing and waning of my feelings instead of thinking through each step. In the process they enabled me to complete a new quilt improvisationally, and to welcome art into my life once and for all.

I began the quilt in the home of my sister-in-law during a summer vacation. I set up my machine on Louise's kitchen table and lovingly stacked the fabrics on the island counter: a perfect set-up. As always, the fabrics drew me into the project. They were the key, the lure into this adventure ahead of me. They acted like a magnet for my soul and we began a dialogue together. I knew nothing of a design, but resolutely forged ahead. I only wanted to combine pulsating indigo blues with burnt oranges in the quilt. I had a fierce longing to interact with them and join them into one vibrant piece.

I focused on a theme of fire and collected quotes associated with it, from Gerard Manly Hopkins, Mary Oliver, Jeremiah's "fire in my bones," the Holy Spirit and phrases from hymns. I remembered also the story from the desert fathers and mothers of the Fourth Century that ended with the words, "Why not become all flame?" I wrote all these down in the journal I keep for noting the progress of my quilts. I placed the journal beside my machine on the kitchen table.

I plunged in by sewing three-inch square "sandwiches" of three layers of orange and blue fabrics, with varying amounts of the two colors. I stitched a design on top, cut down to the next layer, then stitched another design on that layer, and cut down to the bottom layer in a reverse-appliqué process. What a delight to cut through the cloth to the next layer, and the next, and find the vibrant colors beaming up at me. Such fun and energy rivaled only kindergarten play. Consolations prompted me to keep going. When I finished, I had no idea what to do with the forty-three squares, none of them alike.

We moved to another locale to the lovely home of Dan and Sara Juengst set in the languid countryside of South Carolina. I set up an improvised studio again, this time in the library of their guest house. There, I pondered what to do with the squares. I wanted to attach them to a piece of stenciled indigo cloth from Ghana. I thought of arranging them from dark pieces at the bottom progressing to lighter squares at the top. But with Pete's suggestion, I arranged them instead from dark to light toward the center. Then I was faced with how to attach them on the indigo print.

I waited and gazed at the piece in progress. I took my time. I listened to what it had to say to me. I honored its formation. Finally I strung the squares together with embroidery floss and shimmering cords to hang them in five vertical rows, attached only at the top. But what spacing between them? I turned over alternatives in my mind. I eventually bunched them together, with each row slightly overlapping. *Yes!*

I then ruminated over what to do with the orange fabrics which I would arrange in some fashion alongside the blue indigo background piece. I could either stitch (piece) torn strips, or weave them together into a whole piece. When I visited a fabric shop a year before, I had stumbled upon a jacket made of woven strips of fabric. The innovative process struck a chord with me. So I tore long strips of various shades of orange. Tearing fabrics assured a straight line, plus added an interesting texture with the raw edges. I wove them in and out in a laborious, time-consuming process.

I finished the orange section, about the same width as the indigo. I put them side by side on the wall in an asymmetrical balance. The orange overwhelmed the blue, and the viewer. A heavy feeling bore down on me, expressing desolation. I knew I had to make changes. With a sense of agony, I finally concluded that I needed to cut the orange in half, and to attach the two pieces to either side of the blue. I wrote in the quilt journal, *This is where 'commitment' hits the concrete: when you have to revise. Oh, the energy required to do it! Yet, the colors humming in the quilt, the design, the purpose draw me on.*

More questions surfaced. How to attach the orange to the blue? How to fill in gaps? How to quilt the blue section, and then the orange? What colors to back and border the quilt? It would take a time of waiting and pondering between each step to field the answers.

Improvisational art making requires discernment at every step. It requires time. As with most of my quilts, I make no preliminary sketches. Mustering up boldness, I simply make that first cut into fabric. I have no idea what will develop when I begin. Once I find the way to start, I discern which way to go with the design by stopping and listening. In this quilt, I repeatedly waited for a sense of direction to surface, as happened when I strung the squares together, and when I decided to divide the orange into two pieces. With the quilt, I sorted out in my mind the various alternatives. I sifted and weighed. I took my time, trusting the process of creativity to lead the way.

I noticed energetic feelings in one direction and stifling feelings in another — consolations and desolations. One arrangement of the squares felt lifeless, and then another. This weighing with my heart and mind eventually led me to one solution. A pattern emerged when I felt an inner prompting that spoke a resounding *"Yes!"* I had to wait repeatedly for a sense of direction. I groped to find my way. By waiting, listening and then working, I slowly created the quilt, step by step.

Upon finishing the quilt six months later, I named it *Why Not Become All Flame?* It comes from a story to chew on. In the Fourth Century desert, a young monk approaches Abbot Joseph with the question: "What should I do to become more holy? I fast many times a week, I give alms to the poor, I say my prayers eight times a day. What else must I do?" The old abbot stands up and raises his hands to heaven. Fire comes down on all ten of his fingers. He says to the novice, "Why not become all flame?"

The question challenges *me* to become all flame. The question solidifies my realization that fiery passion has directed me into art as it has directed my quilt-making. I therefore needed to throw aside hesitations.

To plunge into the mesmerizing colors. To capture the funky designs dancing in my head. To revel in silk and metallic threads, and glimmering beads of voluptuous hues. To stitch sticks into quilts and pour candle wax on fabrics. To print with onions, buttons, sponges, leaves. To glory in my deep delight and simply let myself go. When I become all flame, when I burn with joyous energy, then — *then* — my art serves others. It feeds the world's hunger. I don't simply share the Good News: I embody it. *Yes!*

**WHY NOT BECOME ALL FLAME?**
28.5" x 24.5"

*"This weighing with my heart and mind led me
to an emerging pattern and an inner Yes!"*

# 5

## CONTEMPLATION IN PRAYER AND ART

꿗

When I ask a group for a definition of "prayer," most people respond: "Communication with God." When we speak of prayer this way, I believe we are locked into *saying* our prayers. We use words praising God, thanking God, confessing to God and interceding for others. I have prayed with words all my life. But somewhere along the way I discovered contemplative prayer which basically is wordless prayer, going beyond communication to commune with God in silence.

This way of praying derives from the definition of contemplation which means an intentional gaze and focus. "To look at something attentively and thoughtfully," says the dictionary. Both contemplative prayer and art making require the ability to focus. No words are used. Our verbal thoughts and speech are laid aside as we intensely focus at length on a particular object. In prayer, the object is connecting with God. In art, the object may be a color or design or a process. When engaged in either one, I become lost in the activity. Other needs, concerns and agendas melt away.

Awareness of my surroundings encourages contemplation. Exuberant wonder in a burgeoning spring time or the fiery energies of autumn becomes wordless prayer which connects me with the Creator. Beauty in nature acts as a lure, drawing me closer to God. In the same way the juxtaposition of colors in my studio often creates a mounting joy when they are just the right sensory combination. In nature, in art, when I notice things, when I truly am focused I find that I become contemplative.

## In a Foreign Land

The seeds of contemplation were sown in mid-life while living in Ghana, and then Nigeria ten years later. All my senses were co-opted for engagement with my foreign surroundings. Different sounds such as the downward trill of the lagoon's kingfisher, distant village drumming, the nightly chant of our Muslim watchman and the intermittent swish, peak and boom of ocean surf not far from our home caught my attention morning, noon and night. Strange smells — some grossly unpleasant — assaulted my senses also. Because everything was new, different, and exciting, I found myself noticing everything.

Ghana was the premier place I began to notice color more intensely. Before Pete and I moved there in 1968 I had imagined our environment would be bland and bleak. Instead I found extravagant beauty. In tropical flowers of hibiscus, flame trees, plumbago and frangi-pangi, in colors of scarlet, blue and yellow. In the market's exuberant displays of limes, papayas, mangoes and pineapples piled together. The colors of tomatoes, purple eggplants and lively okras ricocheting off one another. In vibrant African fabrics splashed in sizzling color combinations along with *kente* cloth which always drew me like a magnet. In nature I reveled in the raging Atlantic Ocean beyond the dark, drooping coconut palms set against the glare of sun on sand. My attempts to capture its vibrancy in watercolors rarely matched the brilliance of real life.

All the mesmerizing colors seeped into my soul. I soaked in the gift of my new surroundings with fresh eyes. A Ghanaian proverb says, "A foreigner has big eyes but will never see everything." Indeed, living on Ghana's coast opened my eyes wide to see as much as possible. I absorbed the new sights, smells and sounds. Such awareness stimulated my senses and made me acutely aware of everything around me.

We lived at the edge of the Atlantic Ocean, four degrees latitude, zero feet in altitude. This meant that it was hot, hot, hot, ameliorated by an occasional sea-borne breeze. With no air conditioning, we managed to get through our days with fans and multiple showers. By each evening, I collapsed. Daylight quickly closed down with an almost audible thud regularly at 7:00 p.m. This meant that my children went to bed early and consistently along with my worn-out husband. It also meant that Ghanaians finished up their business and meetings, and didn't venture out at night. So we didn't either. In our darkened living room I sat alone, awash in ocean's breezes hearing only the watchman's chants and the ping-ping-ping of a fruit bat in our banana tree.

With no TV, telephone or engagements to distract, the evenings offered a rich time for reading — novels as well as spiritual reading — and for prayer. I relished the quiet, the discarding of busyness. I leaned into Presence. At that time, I prayed verbally, in praise, thanksgiving, confession and above all in intercessions to God for others. I believed that prayer was for answers. Many conditions needed addressing, chiefly health concerns in a country where medical facilities often lacked sufficient personnel and equipment. I kept a log of intercessions with answers recorded. It never occurred to me then to pray in any other way. But I relished the silence in those tropical evenings. It acted as a forerunner to contemplative prayer.

We lived in Jos, Nigeria for three years after our sojourn in Ghana at an altitude of about 4000 feet. This meant the climate was much cooler and we weren't so drained of energy by nightfall. But the usual evening silence began to be broken by our children, now teenagers, with their chatter, their homework, and their occasional evening meetings at the nearby American school. The increasing busyness and noise of our lives there hinted that life in the United States would be similar.

In 1982, we returned home and settled into the hustle and bustle of Atlanta, Georgia. This challenged everything in me to stay alive spiritually. Noise and distractions abounded. I became involved in many activities, especially on my road to ordination and becoming an interim minister of a church. Evenings no longer invited solitude and silence. Instead, television, telephones, meetings and our wide-awake teen-agers disrupted them. With firm resolution, I had to carve out a time and place to pray before preparing breakfast. At Villa International where we lived, I resorted to its chapel early in the mornings, sat on cushions, lit a candle and gazed out a long window. One spring time I delighted to see a dove which had made a nest in the curve of a heavy honeysuckle vine up a pine tree. It paralleled my nesting in God. In the silence there, I prayed with better concentration rather than trying to do so after everyone left for work and school, or even trying to pray on-the-go.

### Gleanings from a Retreat

Ten years after our re-entry, visual art began to attract me in my fifties. My eyes opened wide as I was drawn to see in greater depth color and shape in paintings, pottery and fiber art. I began to examine, study and contemplate what I saw in the art world. Such noticing plus an empty time in a retreat I led enhanced my seeing and moved me further toward contemplative prayer and eventually art making.

For the conference center in Montreat, North Carolina, I offered to lead a retreat on creativity. I was itching to weld together ministry and art, even though I considered myself a neophyte in the art world, since at that time, I was only an admirer. After all, such a bold attempt might produce new insights and directions for me since teaching inevitably enriches the teacher. When I read that creativity was a pathway to God, I was determined to explore how to foster this connection. I eventually sifted down my thoughts to a two-fold purpose for the retreat: to help participants to expand their awareness of things around them and of God through focused seeing, and to encourage their creative efforts through simple art making.

I called the retreat "The Eighth Day of Creation," held on an October weekend in 1993. At our opening on Friday night we introduced ourselves, six women and a husband of one of them, stating why we were attracted to a retreat on creativity. All of them expressed desires to explore their creativity; about half had no experiences in art making and expressed somber reservations. Because I had had hesitations about making art, I wanted to assist the timid ones to recover their innate artistic abilities. I also emphasized the safety of our meeting space and offered generous reassurance.

Among the several activities, I included one where we drew a banana without looking down at our paper, moving our pencils as our eyes followed its contours. "We look at things all around us but we never really see them. When we draw an object and give it our unwavering attention we will really see it," I said. Of course our drawings looked nothing like the object in front of us. But they clearly opened our eyes since we intently viewed all the bruises, spots, shadows and curves of the banana as we drew it.

■■■

A major focus of the retreat was an afternoon of fallow time. I spoke of the need for quiet and solitude both in the creative arena and in the spiritual life. With no other agenda for the afternoon, I gave permission to do nothing but to absorb the lovely landscape that Montreat offered by walking in the shadow of the looming mountains, sitting by the lake, or wandering by a noisy creek. Doing nothing, I explained, allows for creative energies and ideas to bubble up. I suggested that the attentiveness we showed in the banana exercise enrich our walking, sitting and noticing. I encouraged sinking into the present moment, noticing beauty, taking delight in nature, and experiencing the presence of God in and around us.

I joined the afternoon of emptiness and wrote in my journal:

*My empty time on creek bank:*
*No noticing the hours slipping away*
*Yet drinking in the proliferation on all sides*

*In leaves, rocks, bugs — endless designs, profuse colors.*

*See how the green rhododendron clusters harbor a tenth golden leaf among them.*

*See the heart-shaped leaves of the spindly plant bursting from the bed of moss.*

*See the fallen pine needles circling where water meets rock.*

*See the gold and green grasses, reflected in the creek in one grand radiance.*

*See the leathery lichens marching up a stick like a ladder.*

*Smile, smile, smile.*

The time beside the creek prompted the beginning of intentional seeing. Not just an occasional glance out my study window to see the shifting sunlight upon leaves and branches. Nor noticing new things as a stranger in a foreign country. But a total absorption and laying aside other concerns. An entering of the space of the object and its entering mine, with distance between us evaporating. I was gazing: being aware of things without judging, without analyzing. Just relishing. Words melted away. I seized the opportunity to be present to Presence with my eyes. I was lost in wonder, love and praise.

Gazing would not have happened if I had not taken the time to sit alone by the creek. Slowing down facilitated a contract with myself to do nothing. Stilling a jar of water so stirred dirt could settle down, I had to still my distractions. Then my mind could clear. My agendas had to fall asleep. I embraced silence. I enjoyed a mini-Sabbath of rest from obligations and concerns. Being on retreat enhanced these possibilities: away from phones, calendars, oughts and musts, I focused on what lay at hand. Brought to a standstill, I walked through mystical doorways to experience the brilliance of God shimmering in nature: the light sifting down on wet leaves, on rushing water. Nature's overflowing gifts became a conduit to communion with the Divine.

Other participants welcomed the fallow time. At retreat's end they expressed their intentions to allow more down time in their hectic lives.

## God in All Things

Ignatius of Loyola proposed that God could be found in all things — a contrary notion in his day when the Church declared that people could encounter God most supremely in the monastery. I found his assertion true at the creek. There I experienced God in the particulars of nature radiant around me, both the similar and the disparate. I reveled in the connections between the spiritual and the material that sprang from gazing. I was beginning to see with the eyes of my heart, beyond the biological and the geological phenomena around me. I affirmed Romans 1: 20: "Ever since the creation of the world God's eternal power and divine nature, invisible though they are, have been understood and seen through the things that God has made."

I thought of lines in Elizabeth Barrett Browning's poem, *Aurora Leigh*, which alludes to Moses' experience at the burning bush:

"Earth's crammed with heaven,
And every bush aflame with God."

Yes, I had found God in the flaming world around me. But then she warns:

"Only those who see take off their shoes,
The rest sit around it, plucking blackberries."

*Only those who see...*welled up in my heart. Yes, I wanted to experience God more fully in my seeing. To contemplate what sits before me in order to access the Divine. To notice all the bushes and trees and flowers aflame with God. To develop a sacramental view of nature. To encourage a sanctified vision. Too often, my awareness clouded over with my busyness, hustle and bustle, and always wanting to do something else instead of just sitting still. I have succumbed to the tyranny of the urgent, putting my hands, mind and will to what lay at hand, usually domestic chores. *Doing* has invariably over-ruled *being*. But now, I wanted to see more deeply, and more consistently. I wanted to take off my shoes in acknowledgement of the Holy One in my life. I wanted to move beyond the compulsive need to pick blackberries.

This deep seeing would take practice — a committed spiritual practice. I would have to push other desires and needs aside and show up regularly for gazing and visual feasting. Not only in the usual places of prayer and worship, not only in nature, but out and about — in human constructions and human beings. I wanted to discipline my eyes to find God in all things. I wanted to pray visually.

Contemplating my surroundings could carry me into prayer like a ferryboat. But I forget. I fail to really see something. It seems that forgetfulness represents the sin that so closely clings to me. The decisive quest of my spiritual life then and now is how to connect with God in the midst of hubbub. To live in the sacrament of the present moment. I have tried to pray while on the go. It's one thing to connect with God in the quiet. But connecting with God in the midst of activity and engagements has tested me the most. Teilhard de Chardin (in the Jesuit fold of Ignatius) claimed that " ...at every moment God awaits us in the activity...at the point of my pen, my pick, my paint brush, my needle — and my heart and my thought...."   This I deeply desired to actualize.

I discovered one way to harness attention. I have resorted to mnemonic devices — placing objects in my path or in my pocket to help me notice and to recollect myself. I use sounds around me to call me to remembrance: bells, chimes, birdcalls, train whistles. This works occasionally. After some disciplined time and effort, contemplation developed in the activity.

Contemplative presence I discovered is a gift. It cannot be manipulated, but I can put myself in a position to let it happen. I did this through a sharpening of what I saw, heard and smelled. I let my senses draw me towards God. Beginning to pay closer attention to common objects around me, I looked for the unusual in the ordinary. I noticed the gold of dawn and the purple of twilight. I noticed the beauty of greens and reds in a head of lettuce. I noticed the different songs that cardinals sing. I noticed the diverse designs of auto hub caps in a parking lot as I walked through it. I noticed the scent of my rosemary bush every time I passed it. I noticed the color of persons' eyes for a change. With greater frequency, I began to anticipate the engagement of my senses, to be open to my surroundings, to be mindful of what is, and to expect surprises. My delight in noticing all these wonders linked me to the presence of God. Being aware of my environment cultivated an awareness of God. One contemplative encounter led to another.

**■ ■ ■**

After I discovered contemplative gazing, using words to pray soon became tedious. I simply did not know what to articulate to God. I only knew that I wanted to be in God's presence. I became restless, so restless that I prayed best when I walked in the mornings at the retirement center down the hill from us. That soon changed.

About this time, I attended a course in spiritual direction at The Oratory, a Catholic center in South Carolina. Before the morning lectures, I prayed as I walked around a small lake behind the house where I stayed. Then we participants gathered for plenary sessions. The atmosphere vibrated with colorful expressions of faith, from laity and clergy, Protestant and Catholic. The stimulating morning lectures were followed by a spiritual direction practicum every afternoon. An evening series focused on St. John of the Cross.

Words associated with John: "union with God," "longing," "dark night," and "the inner eye of love" echoed deep within me. I also learned about John's description of moving from prayer based on thinking and words into contemplative, wordless prayer. "The movement begins when we are unable to relate to God with the mind," the lecturer said. We become dissatisfied with concepts about God, and want only to be with God, sitting still, in silence, in love.

I spoke with him afterward. I described my restlessness yet longing for God. He affirmed that I might be on the contemplative path. His words opened a cache of treasure. I went to the chapel and sat in the dark, without thought of doing, just being. I resolutely focused on the presence of God enfolding me. I paid attention. Distractions seemed to drop away. Tears of joy sprang up. *Tonight*, I wrote in my journal, *You gripped my soul.*

Although I rested in wordless prayer, I found it challenging. I realized that not only preschoolers possess short attention spans — I did, too. Separating myself from all activity and sitting in a quiet, empty space, I found my mind continuing the activity. It was incessantly busy: thinking, planning, remembering, regretting — on and on. I soon discovered that everyone else's minds also constantly chatter. None of us can focus our attention for very long, no matter what our age, no matter what the object. Our thoughts wander all over the place when we try to corral them. Even the sense of God's presence seems to vanish sporadically. When contemplation fails me — and it most certainly will from time to time because of human finiteness — I cannot beat myself over the head. I need to trust the slow work of God. I cannot become contemplative in an instant. Remembering that I can never give God my full attention, it is my intention that matters. This thought helps settle me down.

In my day-to-day life, I made contemplative prayer a priority. I allowed time for emptiness. Once again my eyes began to pull me into contemplation with its intense and steady focus. I began to put objects in my prayer space: a candle, a stone, a leafy branch which my eyes gazed upon. Again as at Montreat's creek, there was a mutual entering of space, I with the object and it with me. This wordless, visual experience opened the door to God. I was praying through my eyes. This led to praying with icons of the Eastern Church.

## Icons

When we lived in Ghana, I had first discovered icons but not in the traditional sense. Although the vigorous coastline captivated me with its beauty, I missed mountains, rivers, and seasons. Someone, however, sent us a subscription to *Wonderful West Virginia*, a periodical loaded with gorgeous colored photos of the scenery I missed: drooping tree limbs over a meandering stream, the colors of dawn caught in a frozen pond, frosted maple leaves. I cut out the photos and tacked them to a bulletin board in our bedroom. Years before that interlude beside Montreat's creek, I was experiencing the lure of beautiful nature as a conduit to God. At great length, I gazed at the photos lovingly. My spirit somehow lifted in doing so. Through the photos of the captivating scenery I mysteriously began to experience the transcendent. They acted as windows to God, which is the definition of icons.

Traditional icons of the Eastern Church depict saints and biblical figures, painted in prescribed ways. The figures appear distorted. Their irregular features intentionally try to convey a spiritual reality, not a physical one. Their eyes loom large, noses and mouths are thin and minimally rendered. Gold paint suggests mystery and holiness of the person depicted. Icons do not serve a decorative purpose on a wall or in a book. They normally support worship; they invite prayer. Through my eyes I encounter the painted eyes. They affirm that the presence of God can be experienced not only by the ear but by the eye. I begin to see, not in the sense of understanding some thing or some one. But to see with my inner being, to *see* in order to experience the touch of God.

I bought an icon of Jesus at a Greek festival in Atlanta. The eyes of Jesus invited me into his space. They spoke to me, encouraged me, and evoked intimacy. His presence was made more real through my eyes.

A few years later, in a Catholic gift shop, I bought a copy of the Virgin of Vladimir, also called the Virgin of Tenderness. It enhanced my view of icons and their usefulness in my life. In this icon, the baby Jesus' arm encircles his mother's neck, and his cheek lies next to hers. Additionally, the virgin's left hand motions to the viewer to enter love's embrace. Truly, in this portrayal, love is made visible. It spills out from the icon and into my spirit. The baby's cheek touches *mine*; his arm encircles *my* neck, the virgin invites *me* to share their communion. I am immediately engulfed in a sense of love whenever I come into its presence.

Another icon, a reproduction of Rublev's Holy Trinity, conveys love to me as well. This icon, with its graceful, luminous figures bending towards one another sitting at table, portrays a gentleness and a sense of communal intimacy. The lovely gold and aqua colors arrest my attention. An empty space at the table, front and center, invites me, the viewer, to sit with the three. The figure on the right with its finger pointing down at the table seems to say to me, *Sit right here, and keep silence.* The icon's serenity draws me into the circle of love time after time. I pray with it from Pentecost to Advent, and the Vladimir icon from Advent to Pentecost.

Gazing at icons — as with nature — halts my thoughts and stills my need for verbal expression. If I can minimize analyzing and verbalizing I can experience pure being. Thoughts and words instead of reinforcing my contact with God more often fracture it. Certainly, all of us are prone to analyze, categorize and organize what we see with our eyes, and then use words to make sense with each other. We do it all the time to get through the day. But to close the door on my usual verbal puzzles and concerns opens up a space. In it, I don't have to prove anything to anybody, or struggle with the right words at the right time. I rest in God in my time of prayer, allowing God's compelling love to draw me even closer.

## Lectio Divina

In my practice of contemplative prayer, I begin by lighting a candle or two before an icon. I quiet myself, sometimes with music. The visual and the auditory presences lead me into a sacred dimension. I then follow an ancient prayer form called *lectio divina:* sacred reading. It basically means to pray the scriptures. First I read a selected portion of Scripture slowly and sometimes out loud. Second, I chew on its meaning, especially its meaning for me. How does this reading intersect my present context? What questions is it asking of me? After considering the implications for awhile, in the third step I then respond to God in prayer. Sometimes, the reading points to an anxiety, or a lack of trust, or un-forgiveness. In a verbal prayer I respond to God about my discoveries.

The fourth step in *lectio* is a contemplative resting. I let go my wordy thoughts and absorb God's presence. I cry in the words of the hymn, *The Lone Wild Bird,* "I am thine, I rest in thee; Great Spirit, come, and rest in me." Amazingly, the restlessness I once experienced has abated as I sit, resting in God.

My thoughts still run wildly all over the place. I need to view my thoughts like a boat going down a river which I must resist boarding. I have to let them go. To focus on God alone requires an anchor of sorts to keep me centered. When my mind wanders, I use a word to bring me back to my intention, sometimes "Yesu," or simply, "Yes." I do this whenever my thoughts capture me during the twenty minutes or so devoted to prayer. The process can be a struggle. It requires discipline not to get up and leave. In between the calling back of thoughts to the focus of attention are moments of emptiness. Here God can touch me in ways beyond my understanding. I close with intercessions for the day and a short verbal prayer of commitment.

Instead of *lectio divina* I can also engage in *imaginatio divina*, a visual rendition of the prayer form. It means gazing at an object which captures my attention, savoring each aspect of shape, line and color. By doing nothing but seeing I let it draw me into the presence of God. When my mind wanders, I bring it gently back to the image I have encountered. Second, I try to understand how the object may be telling me something — about myself, life, or God. It may connect me to a concern in my life, an issue. Third, I respond with prayer to God, making an offering of any discovery. Last, I rest quietly and openly in God's loving presence.

I thought I was off track as I practiced contemplative prayer when images bubbled up in my mind along with thoughts. Behind my closed eyelids, colors and abstract patterns swirled. Sometimes I saw the specific layout for a quilt. I resisted the temptation to duplicate the image on paper. I felt it would disrupt the prayer and the silence. After all, I was here to commune with God, not to compose art. Still, I wondered: why the visual images?

Author Eric Maisel resolved my puzzle. He speaks of the beginning stages of creativity as a process of *hushing and holding*. We have a burning desire to create, he says, but where do we go from there? He suggests that we grow quiet inside. Hush our thoughts. Concentrate on breathing. *Go silently into the darkness.* There in the darkness, he promises, ideas of melodies, images, lyrics will come. Then cling to the idea or image that has special vitality. As it grows more distinct in the dark silence, hold it and nurture it. Then do whatever it takes to bring it to life, in words, images, music or movement.

Indeed, artistic creativity arises from the same source as prayer. Connecting with both God and our creative self springs from that fertile inner darkness, the stillness of our centered souls. I need not discount the images that arise in my prayerful moments, or fret that something is "wrong." In their time and place, they have a worthwhile purpose. If art and prayer are conceived in my inner depths, I believe that my art making takes on a sacred dimension. The images when birthed help express my encounter with God because such an encounter cannot be verbalized. How can I possibly speak of wonder and mystery? How does one share the inner depths of feeling to another? How is mystical experience communicated? How does one visualize the inner fire? Words simply flounder within any significant experience — such as falling in love, or giving birth to a baby or relating to God.

I believe I can share the ineffable primarily through images. I express the inexpressible in my creative artistic efforts. Judith Rock, dancer, said: "There are ideas, insights and experiences which only sound can communicate, others only communicated by movement, others which only color and line can capture. This is why the arts offer insight into God, each other and ourselves which can be offered in no other way." No wonder in the dark silence of contemplation and in the ambience of prayer, images danced in my mind's eye. As a visually oriented person I see visual images when I am centered. Our creative God uses many means to reach us and we have to use many to respond. Words are one avenue, images another.

## Stitched to God

As artists, when we engage in our art work we become contemplative. We pay attention to shape and color, line and rhythm. We gaze at possibilities. Our focus narrows to the project at hand. We tune out distractions. I clearly understood this phenomenon of attentiveness in my next quilt. It was birthed in contemplative moments.

Initially, the process of working out the design involved ideas, analysis and decisions. Options confronted me, as to fabrics, shapes, and colors. I settled on small squares, rectangles and a few triangles from three swatches of decorator fabrics a friend had given me. I cut out those areas in the fabric that looked like watercolor washes in shades of green, burgundy, pink and creamy white. Then I arranged the pieces in a path from the dark reds and greens to the white at the top right corner. I labored over blending the colors from one shape to the next with no abrupt change. It felt like putting together the pieces of a giant jigsaw puzzle.

I sewed a few of the pieces in place with a curving line of red embroidery swooping up from the lower left hand corner to the upper right. The rest of the pieces I fastened to the backing by hand with beads: dozens of beads, sewed in almost every corner of the geometric shapes. The beading required inserting invisible nylon thread into an almost invisible eye of a skinny needle. Threading the needle and knotting the thread proved challenging. It frequently knotted and I'd have to start over. I then drew it up from the backing to the front into the hole of the bead, and down to the back again several times to secure the bead. Up and down. Up and down. Bead after bead after bead, day after day after day.

Analysis faded; contemplation took hold when the quiet repetitive action of my hands allowed my inner self to grow quiet. Every other part of my life fell away when I gave the quilt my full attention, time and energy. I was thoroughly focused, totally absorbed. Not reflecting, not considering what to do next, not ruminating, just absorbed. The repetitive process captured my body and mind, heart and spirit. In and out, up and down. Over and over again. My mind was stilled, my verbalizing halted, and with the stillness, God's presence enfolded me. "Hands to work, hearts to God," the Shaker saying came alive. In communion with God, I was praying through my work, my hands, my eyes. Sewing the beads centered me. Stitching the beads stitched me to God.

How do I communicate this contemplative moment in quilting? In these words I have tried, but they fall short. The quilt itself expresses far more than I can.

*The magnetic dark burgundies and greens*
*Melting into light*
*pinks and gold;*
*The curving upward progression of the dark red*
*Embroidery woven with gold metallic thread;*
*The abundance of glowing beads — these speak*
*Of a dawning awareness of God*
*In the work:*
*God in the creative endeavor,*
*God in the*
*Visual imagery.*
*I named the quilt "O Radiant Dawn".*
*The title not only reflects*
*The darkness-into-light of Advent.*
*It discloses my own dawning that*
*God is in*
*All things,*
*Including my art.*

**O RADIANT DAWN**
27.5" x 37"

*"With the repetitive up and down motions of stitching, I became stitched to God."*

# 6
## CREATION INVIGORATES MY ART

❧❦

### Flaming Beauty

For three radiant months in the autumn of 1994, I served as chaplain at Ghost Ranch, a Presbyterian conference center sixty-six miles north of Santa Fe, New Mexico. Pete drove us westward to drop me off. When he left, I saw his car weaving in and out the curves of the road, and I unexpectedly cried. Already I missed his bear hugs, his laughter, and the way he filled up empty spaces in my life.

After dinner, I frequently walked around Ghost Ranch's pungent alfalfa field, recently mown. Down the road the yellow-gold *chamisas* greeted me, their feathery heads glowing. Into the yellows of the tall stalks and heads a clump of purple flowers intruded and set up vibrations, shooting joy into the air. In the valley running up to Pedernal Mountain, the rills and ridges tipped with green and blue, melted into the sun's last light. Strands of golden light inter-laced the ridges, beckoning, calling, *Go green, deep down inside*, they seemed to say to me. *Come alive! Shimmer yourself in the golden dust of twilight. Revel in Jupiter and Venus hanging like lanterns in the dusky blue. Walk in beauty.*

The landscape seemed to march on forever. It drew me out of my urban co-coon. My stale soul, cramped from city living, felt sprung from restrictions. The limitless vista pulled a longing out of me I couldn't name. My soul expanded with the space and dissolved into it. Like a butterfly, my wings of creativity, vitality and delight unfolded. Here I am, totally me with no excess baggage to identify who I am. I am strictly God's child lost in wonder and praise.

Behind me, Kitchen Mesa's red cliffs faded in the sunlight, ignited by fiery sparks from the western sky. Deep red, Indian red, permanent red, earthy, brick red, where energy burns and nature's furnace simmers and never abates, never dies out. All that fieriness overflowed into me, and I became invigorated because of the raw energy aflame in the cliffs. The redness enkindled and enlivened me. I sloughed off the dead skin of my same-old-same-old city self. The space and sky, the red cliffs and exotic flora began to re-create me.

At night, when I walked, the moon or the stars illumined my path. I could see deer feeding in the alfalfa field, their eyes gleaming from the muted light. Occasionally, a distant coyote's call punctured the silence. I inhaled the stillness and reveled in its peace. Back home, I was encumbered with the city's insistent noise of car motors, horns, and brakes on pavement. At the Ranch, I fell into the arms of silence with one exception. Shortly after my arrival, some conferees of men drummed up on the mesa. Their beating splintered the sky, showering streams of moonlight down upon the Ranch below. The drums throbbed from my toes to my hairline and quickened my heart to pulse to their rhythm. Encircled by drumming under the moonlit sky, I melted into the red canyons and mesas.

## Empty Hours, Lonely Days

Set down alone in this geographical wonder, I quickly assessed past and present. Before my arrival, I despaired of my overflowing commitments. *One project spawns another; one committee spins out more and more to do*, I wrote in my journal. I also noted the sparse hours I spent per week on my art or my writing. Two here, three there, never more than four. "Oh, God!" I moaned.

"What would my life look like if I were in charge of it?" Nancy Chinn's voice resounded in my ears. This new locale would enhance my taking charge. I had escaped my compacted days of pressures and expectations. I had turned my back on my calendar, phone and occasionally my clock. Even back-home relationships were temporarily cut. Severing my moorings, I drifted in waters unmarked by appointments and meetings. The clean slate of each day unmarked with a to-do list challenged me. Initially, I felt I was floating in an endless sea of languor. Only the hours for meals, for Sunday worship and for occasional volunteer activities marked my time. I had to structure everything else and order the hours of the day. The basic job description called me "worship coordinator." I saw myself in a broader capacity. Beyond Sunday worship I mixed and mingled with Hispanics and Anglos, becoming acquainted, listening and observing. Where appropriate, I offered pastoral presence among staff and conferees.

I developed a schedule of sorts, weaving private, contemplative moments in my room or on walks followed by outer involvements. In early morning hours, I prayed, wrote, and followed Julia Cameron's exercises in *The Artist's Way*. Then I interacted with others the rest of the day: in leading Sunday worship services, helping in the mail room and the Trading Post, and engaging conferees and staff in the dining room. On Mondays I washed my clothes and camped in the library's room of extensive biblical and theological books to work on a sermon. I studied and took notes for three days. By Thursday I began to type up the sermon and had it ready so, by Saturday, I could post notices around the Ranch about the forthcoming Sunday worship.

Although the use of my time challenged me, it paled in contrast to my confrontation with loneliness. I had forgotten how moving to a strange neighborhood jerked one back to a childlike existence, into the dilemmas of newness: when and where to eat the next meal, where to wash clothes, where to find what, and who was who. At the Ranch, I was the un-named, unknown stranger learning the fundamentals of acquaintanceship. I didn't know anything about anybody else nor did they about me. No one had a clue about my identity, what to expect of me, and what I had to offer. Queries at meals surfaced briefly: "Where are you from?" "Have you been here before?" "Are you attending a conference?" After I answered the three questions, the inquirers moved on. They habitually turned to each other to share mutual interests. I was left alone to view the assortment of people in the dining room. In the newness, the others had to take me at face value. What they saw of me was what they got — an impression, until time and common tasks proved otherwise.

I assuaged my need for companionship by retreating to the well-stocked library every evening. Books became my intimate friends. I read novels and poetry, and absorbed books on women's issues, on Southwest Native American and Hispanic cultures, art, creativity, and spirituality, plus the biblical and theological books I had discovered in sermon writing. The library hosted such a feast of books and periodicals I had trouble making choices. Each spoke deeply to me, embraced me, and warmed me.

Upon finding *Women Who Run with the Wolves*, I read that Clarissa Pinkola Estes says to create, one must be surrounded by warm, supportive friends. Otherwise, we resort to daydreams and our creative life freezes. *How in the world will I ever be able to create or write or paint in this environment?* I wrote. *How can I sing the Lord's song in a strange land...this desert land?*

The Ranch sits on 24,000 acres in high desert country. In Ghana and Nigeria I viewed myself living in a metaphorical desert. I discovered then that the desert has a way of stripping anyone who ventures into it. It did me. In Africa, I learned slowly to do without and to make do with things at hand. Activities, busyness, and material things melted away. Friendships flowered and kept me alive. But I constantly felt that there was no meaningful project to write home about.

Projects. How I and every other compatriot are consumed with projects. How our lives revolve around them. At a conference, an astute Ghanaian had observed that we Americans are project-oriented, not person-oriented as Africans are. If I have no project, what is my worth? What I do and what I accomplish tend to identify me. But in their stripping away while in Africa, my relationship with God thrived.

Re-entering the desert at Ghost Ranch, I was divested of an abundance of material goods, relationships, projects or the lures of nearby towns. Very little distracted me. Upon thumbing through the Bible, I resonated with the psalmist's question: "Can God spread a table in the wilderness?" (Ps. 78:19)

I investigated the Bible's further references to the desert. How did the people of that day survive desert living? Prophets, the Israelites, even Jesus regarded the desert as a place of refuge. By meeting no competitors in its vast emptiness, they experienced God. They responded to God's call. Hosea referred to the time of wilderness wanderings as a honeymoon period of intimate closeness between Israel and their God. Perhaps, I, too, could view this desert time as a fruitful one — a time of discovering new aspects of my life and putting down deep spiritual roots. I could become more enmeshed in God.

■ ■ ■

On Sunday afternoons, in my solitude I reveled in the world, resplendent around me. Sunday morning worship revitalized me as it always did. I experienced both privilege and power in sharing the Gospel with others, even with the small handful who attended. But after lunch and a nap, Sunday afternoons sucked the morning's energy from me. With the offices, the Trading Post, the mail room, the museums closed, I, too, felt shut down. Apart. Nonfunctional. Drifting. Relating to no one.

So I explored the world around me. I took long, contemplative walks in which I noticed everything. I stopped time after time to look, to listen, to touch, to ingest, and to inhale the pungent aromas of sage and piñon spiking the air.

The walks began on the road bordered by cottonwood trees, their yellow heart-shaped leaves fluttering overhead. The golden *chamisas* on both sides, shoulder high, waved at me. They stood like spectators at a parade turning to look who's coming next. *It is I, only me, alone, walking softly, walking hesitantly, in awe,* I mused. Only the twitters of tiny gold-tinged birds disrupted the stillness. The sage bushes, brassy colored and taller than I, drew me to their captivating scent. I swished and swayed with willows, grasses and cattails by a pond, as I searched for the source of rippling water. I am one with the water, with the reeds, with the cliffs. I am of them, and they of me. The Creator's hand and the Creator's raw material connect us all. I craned my neck to view the cliffs, their rosy-redness heaved up from hidden depths. They grazed the edge of cerulean sky, high and free, majestic and timeless. Somehow the butte's ancient towering pulled me back and back into the beginnings of things, and I was at one with time and creation. I pondered what lay in their crevices: potshards? Ravens' nests? Human remains? When I walked farther into the canyon where the cliff walls slowly converge, I was in their grip and there was no escaping their awesome immutability.

In this new and unfamiliar garden spot of creation, I savored everything around me. Nature nurtured me. It restored my soul and became my needed companion. I perceived a splendor on all sides. The "eye of my eye is opened," as ee cummings wrote, and I overflowed with wonder, mystery and gratitude.

I had been brought face-to-face with radiant nature before. I had seen God shining through it, at Montreat's creek and in the light sifting through the trees outside my Atlanta home. But this experience of nature at Ghost Ranch differed from previous ones. Granted, the arid desert contrasted sharply with the verdure of the southeast. As in Ghana, the Ranch's novelty drew me to notice everything. In this setting and in my isolation, however, noticing nature's gifts imparted a new and nurturing presence. I felt enfolded by it. I was drinking in the river of God's delights, ecstatic with God's art work. I soon realized that the Creator was reaching out through glowing creation to cradle me in my loneliness. I experienced joy in new patterns and vibrant colors in cliffs and sky. The great expansiveness of the desert re-created me. The natural beauty of the Ranch was God's personal gift to me. As with any gift given, I, as the recipient, felt treasured. In nature's presence, vision and purpose washed over me. I re-affirmed my identity as God's beloved.

## Creative Fire Re-kindled

About a month into my stay, I had a disturbing dream. I dreamed of being dragged somewhere by a sinister man. He pulled me into a bus and sat next to me, gripping my arm. I couldn't escape him. Two young men — one blonde, one brunette — saw my plight, sat behind us and choked him. I was free, but terrified, and woke up in a panic. In her book, Clarissa Pinkola Estes said that dreams of the sinister man are sent to wake up our smoldering creative fire, so we will take our gifts, our art, and our creativity more seriously. The dreams point us to whatever is squelching our creativity. In my case — as she so well described — the over-commitments of my city life had stolen my fire. She advises a woman to protest strongly against consuming responsibilities because "Art is not meant to be created in stolen moments only. They will rob her of her creativity," she says. *She seems to be peering into my life*, I acknowledged. Then later, she says, when we lose focus, the thing to do is just sit down, be still and peel away the commitments that have bound us. When we focus we use our intuition, and stop, look, smell, listen, feel and taste. She said that women can claim their voices, values and imaginations from the world around them.

At Ghost Ranch I was definitely not over-committed. My responsibilities did not swallow me up as they did back home. I had time to be still and use my intuition. I certainly became tuned to the world around me to claim its values. I began to be truly focused, primarily on my desert surroundings which engaged all of my senses.

Eventually, I could not contain the ecstasy flowing from this newfound world. It pressed within me when I awoke every morning to raven's wings beating past my window. It hovered over me as I walked the Ranch's dusty roads. I inhaled it when golden twilight wrapped around me. As a result I was propelled toward art making. With urgency I took out my watercolors. I wanted my exorbitant feelings to pour into concrete visual expressions. I wanted to return a morsel of beauty to the Creator who had lavished it on me. The expanse of sky and endless terrain pulled out of me the inner necessity to create. The red cliffs ignited my inner fire. My love for the creation revitalized my creativity.

I painted golden, heart-shaped cottonwood leaves. I discovered how to move the paint around to make the leaves glow from the center. I called the painting *Inner Radiance*.

I painted purple mesas pulsating against a sunset's flaming sky.

I painted the misty tamarisk bush at my doorstep, washing blues, greens and yellows across the paper.

I found the joy of painting feelings and impressions, not representations. In my journal I wrote: *I paint because I must. Because this exquisite, exuberant energy must find an outlet. I am impelled to harness the ecstasy, to ring in the joy! Paint because I must, or I will burst.*

I painted out of gratitude. I painted with exuberance. My art making became my prayer of thanksgiving.

The sinister man of the frightening dream indeed had shaken me. He along with the luminous offerings of the world re-kindled my creative fire.


## God Revealed in Nature

In the Ranch library I found saints and mystics who, like me, experienced God in nature: Meister Eckhart. Francis of Assisi. William Blake. Teilhard de Chardin. I was amazed that the Christian Celts (2nd through 7th centuries) declared that God was revealed in two books: the book of Holy Scripture and the book of nature. They saw every component of creation as a manifestation of God, as a sacrament. Because their livelihood depended on the natural forces around them, the Celts understood this linkage. In their attentiveness, "...there is a shudder in our blood when we see the traces of [God's] crafts-man's hands upon the world...", as quoted by Esther de Waal from a Welsh poem in her book about the Celtic tradition.

Hildegard of Bingen (12th Century) also absorbed nature intently and wrote of it, putting to use its herbs and plants for medicinal purposes. She lived in the lush, verdant landscape of Germany's Rhine River and often spoke of the "greening power of the Holy Spirit" (*viriditas*), who animated the life of every living thing. She wrote:

> I, the highest and fiery power, have kindled every living spark and I have breathed out nothing that can die.... I flame above the beauty of the fields; I shine in the waters, in the sun, the moon and the stars. I burn. And by means of the airy wind, I stir everything into quickness with a certain invisible life which sustains all.... I, the fiery power lie hidden in those things and they blaze from me.

I savored the words of these nature mystics. I was not alone: my Christian tradition supported me. In my joyful praise of and contentment with the natural world, I felt accompanied by those who had also felt the presence of God in their habitats. For, I also "shuddered in [my] blood" at the glories of creation. I, too, had been touched by the flaming beauty of the mesas, fields and red cliffs. I relished all my discoveries in God's gifts to me during that autumn at Ghost Ranch.

## Assisting God

In spite of beauty in creation, a dark side also exists. When we examine the creation we find that things are not quite right: changes need to be made. A chaotic element intertwines with beauty which we humans, we caretakers need to remedy or reform where we can. The world must be shot through with new life or else we will all be dragged down to the pit through neglect, extinction and violence. God is working toward resurrection in small, slow, and sometimes hidden ways. God tamed the chaos in Genesis One, and does also today, usually with our aid.

Because my love for God's world flamed higher, I wanted to protect it. I could not bear the thought of such beauty deteriorating. With my deep love for nature, how could I strive to preserve it in its glory rather than trampling on it? Would this be a question I would pose in future artistic creations?

I, too, enter into this effort to align myself with God's purposes in so small a way as when I restore my home to order or create loveliness in a floral bouquet. My imagination, ability, and energy to create continue the process that God set in motion in the story of creation in Genesis One and Two. For reasons none of us can fathom, God cannot do without the human family. Mysteriously, I am continuing God's work in the cosmos in what some call "the eighth day of creation," through what Hildegard says we are called to do: assist God.

In the biblical creation story, God asks for the human's assistance in naming the creatures brought before him. The human is also commissioned to nurture and protect the earth. God does not do it. God created the first man and woman but did not create subsequent human creatures. God gave human beings the ability to reproduce their own kind in order to continue God's creative work. In other words, God drew back some of God's creative powers and invested them in men and women. In me. In you. Creation continues by means of my creativity and yours, which, joining with hosts of others' efforts, assists the development of the world's greatest potential. By extending God's work in the world, we can be called co-creators with God.

Co-creators with God. The term sounds almost too grandiose for me. How can I elevate myself to such a position? But truthfully, God has done this, not I. My creativity is derived from God's. Because I am created, I am creative. I am God's agent in the world, commissioned to care for the creation and to be "fruitful and multiply" (Gen. 1:28) which goes far beyond reproduction. Fruitfulness is the outcome of creativity. We are being fruitful when we make any new thing: when we organize, visualize, build, renovate, dance, sing or paint house or canvas. God empowers us through creative energies to use our gifts and abilities, for the sake of others and for the good of creation. Not just artistic gifts, not just the fruits of  poetry, painting, sculpture or musical composition. The arts form part of a continuum. Some gifts give meaning and beauty to lift the viewer beyond the mundane. Other gifts secure and sustain the creation. We are all artists in one form or another.

Harnessing my ecstasy through artistic visual attempts, I work in sync with the Creator. In the paintings I rendered at Ghost Ranch, I co-created with God. I made something new. I assisted God by attempting to mirror God's art through my art making. In my joyful painting of the Southwestern landscape, I wanted the joy to spill out to viewers. I offered to God my heartfelt gratitude for the gift of creation and for my beginning ability to reflect in paint my feelings towards many of its treasures.

As I painted, I experienced being "in the flow." Some other creative force, inspiration, and energy poured through me. Time, the space in which I worked and even a grumbling empty stomach went unnoticed. While in deep concentration, I was one with the work, and it with me. An accelerated exuberance and energy in painting gripped me. I felt attuned and alive with the whole universe. My soul expanded as if to hear the planets singing, and to see the *chamisas* dancing.

God was re-creating me in the artistic process. God was directing me by tapping into my creative energies. I could not resist the fiery passion to paint which continually drew me into God's longing for me and pointed out my path.

In awe, I gazed at *Inner Radiance* and inwardly remarked *Where did this come from?* The design, the color, the mood did not originate entirely with me or my imagination. The Spirit seemed to flow through me as I put paint on paper to re-create the subject that had so transfixed me. It was as if I had "made of my life a simple flute" as Indian poet Rabindrinath Tagore has said, through which God's melody had poured out of every hole. I was the instrument, the channel. Is this not the ecstasy of creativity — to receive from God and give back to God? Not that my results reflected the perfection of the Creator. In my hesitant strokes and watercolor muddles, I was gleefully birthing something new into the world that had not yet come into existence. And it came into existence with my personal stamp imposed on it.

My creative efforts and yours are unique because we have been uniquely created. When we offer our gifts in harmony with each other something beautiful can be born. Each of us has something unique to share that no one else can emulate. Each of us is compelled to create at different stages of life, young or old even during illness and disability, or retirement, or grief, or job loss. Outlook, vision, and energy are peculiar to me and peculiar to you. No one else expresses the same gifts and abilities that I do. I paint or quilt — or write or preach, or walk or talk, or construct — as only I can.

## The Creative Process

I have noticed, along with artists of all kinds, stages of the creative process. From my mental rumination over a sketchy project to the completed, tangible piece, one stage follows another as I bring to life my imaginative ideas. At times, some stages are skipped; some repeated. The stages may even seem to spiral around, bringing me back to the beginning. It is important to realize that *frustration* is one of the stages so I do not lose heart. Inevitably, I come across it when I hit a level of uncertainty or darkness, but I cannot let it deter me.

My next quilt brought me through the stages. The *preparation* stage began when I was drawn to a milky bead with a barely discernable bird-like figure embedded in it. I picked it out and warmed it in my hand. *Did I choose it, or did it choose me? Did the work which grew around the bead wait for me to birth it?* I wondered. In addition to the bead, I found pieces of dark blue-green fabric with white dots swirling around. To me, they reflected the movement of wind. In the bead and in the small fabric pieces, I visualized creation spinning out of the spirit-wind-breath of God.

With creation as a possible theme, I began to brainstorm how to do the quilt. Through a spontaneous visit with a friend, the quilt announced a definite direction when she gave me fabric for its top. It consisted of a lovely aqua damask from Senegal, West Africa. The friend had been a missionary nurse in

Africa most of her life. She had invited me to bring my *Transformation* quilt to her home. When we finished talking about it, she went to a chest of drawers and pulled out the damask. "I don't need this," she said, "and neither does my daughter. Here, you take it. You need it," and dropped all shimmering nine yards of it into my lap. I barely found my voice to thank her for this affirming gift.

The damask, the bead, the stormy pieces of fabric decided my color scheme in the cool blues, greens and aquas of sky, earth and sea. Starting with these colors, I pulled out pieces of fabrics from my stash, and strewed them around my work room to audition them. As with the beginning of all my quilts, this stage consisted of a nothing-nailed-down openness as I contemplated many directions for the quilt. I had to proceed step by step, not knowing clearly where I was to go as I tried various color combinations together. I simply responded improvisationally to each possibility as it arose with a Yes or No feeling in my gut.

When all the options are out on the table, that's when *frustration* sets in. With the vast array of fabrics surrounding me in my studio, I felt frozen to make choices. Enticing ones lay everywhere I looked but I couldn't choose them all! I had to narrow down my options. How could I possibly leave out this luscious green, or the turquoise with the little yellow dots, or the embroidered chartreuse? I moved fabrics around, overlapping one with another to see how they interacted. I discarded this one and chose that one, but placing the two with a third sometimes created a clash. I started over again, repeatedly. It took me days to decide. When I finally did, I faced another hurdle. What was I going to do with them? What was the entry point that would begin to bind together this lively array of fabrics? My design remained unfocused, my outcome nebulous, my resolve shaky. At this stage I wrote in my journal: *My heart in my stomach. Swamped in self-doubt. Can I really make another quilt? Is there anything new in me to produce one? ...Fearful.*

I had to let the matter rest and not be overwhelmed with the confusing multiplicity of possibilities. I had to let *incubation* take over. I had to breathe deeply and trust that my next steps would present themselves at the right time. At this stage, I've discovered that long walks help relieve the strain of indecision. Domestic chores — like gardening or cleaning house — also present a different focus and sometimes trigger what to do next. Putting the mind out to pasture allows the mysterious forces of creativity to do their work. Unbelievably, simply resting from the project enables it to move ahead. Creative directions often emerge during a fallow time. Intuition has a chance to grow. While in the frustration stage, believing that rest from the project will gain direction requires considerable trust in the process. I rested for a month, hanging on to trust with my fingernails. Making this quilt helped me value the experience of letting go and braced me during the incubation stages of future quilts.

*Illumination* arrives next in a great *A-ha!* moment. This sudden insight cannot be engineered but I can open myself to its arrival. If I trustingly wait and expect a resolution it will come. If I remain open and notice things, ideas will pop up anywhere. Books, events, displays, nature, others' quilts and my own quilts invite illumination to emerge from the shadows. My breakthrough came when I saw in a book a paper collage of woven strips. Inspecting my *Flame* quilt hanging on a bedroom wall confirmed the process. As I scrutinized its section of orange strips woven in and out of each other in that quilt, I knew then what I must do with the new quilt. I would weave torn strips of fabric on top of the aqua damask, symbolizing God's weaving the creation from nothing.

At last, I knew where to go with the quilt and with which fabrics. Then began the period of hard work to put it together, the stage of *perspiration*. I had found a pattern of aqua, yellow-green and dark blue for the backing. I placed it and then the batting on my design wall. On top of these I laid the damask on which I placed the torn strips from fabrics I had finally chosen. Some of the strips were prints, some were pieces of African embroidery from my husband's *dashiki* long since worn out, one came from a batik print of a pants suit made for me in Ghana. All of them came in hues of blues, dark turquoises, greens and yellow-greens, with intermittent fuchsia pieces acting as zingers in shapes of objects driven by the wind: kites and sails. All the pieces were placed on top of the aqua — *A gorgeous, energizing, vibrant mix!* I wrote. There's no turning back now.

The weaving took forever. I then added figures in the spaces between the strips: the charm of a star, a scarab bead, fabric images of a dolphin and a flowered garden, and hand-made stencils of a bird and then a man and woman holding hands. Hand stitching fuchsia and aqua cording and embroidering great circles of stitches emanating from the milky bead followed. People often ask quilters, "How long did it take you to make your quilt?" Most of us can only estimate the time. But to pinpoint an actual time frame for part of this quilt, I figured it took four hours just to complete one large circle of hand-sewn embroidery.

When I stepped back from the finished quilt I again questioned *Where did this come from? Did I really execute the work?* I believe that awe embraces this stage of creation I felt as if some other force poured through me to make the quilt. I felt that the wind-breath-spirit (*Ruach* in Hebrew) herself was the instigator. God was behind and in the impulse; I acted merely as the mid-wife. I had responded with heart, hands and mind to the call to create. My responsibility was simply to show up at the work table. God's spirit — directing, enabling, confirming — did the rest. I assisted God in the process. I became God's servant to do the work. I became a co-creator with God. I luxuriated in the finished quilt which featured my favorite blend of colors. With great satisfaction I hung it in our apartment. I named it *Ruach: Weaving the Creation.*

The *communication* stage of creativity followed. This must be the natural outcome of our creative work. Our gifts are meant to be shared. God gives them, and we give them back to God in a circle of giving. In the process, onlookers are enriched by our work. We must invite viewers in to see our creations. Make no mistake. Any scribble on paper, any doodle on the piano can support someone else's life at a particular time or place. Who am I to say this piece doesn't matter, and refuse to display it? It doesn't have to be *high art*, but just a heartfelt visual expression of my inner self. My God-given imagination and gifts have brought the work to life. I therefore present it for the common good, not out of self-aggrandizement but because the creative spirit in my work impels me to communicate it.

I shared *Ruach* in various exhibits, some juried, some not. I gained the most pleasure seeing it hang at the entrance of the Continuing Education building of my Seminary in an exhibit entitled *New Beginnings.* The exhibit heralded the installation of the Seminary's new president.

**RUACH: WEAVING THE CREATION**
41" x 50.5"

*"In beginning the quilt, I was drawn to
a mysterious milky bead.
Did I choose it? Or did it choose me?"*

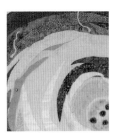

# 7

# SEEDS OF PAST ARTISTIC ATTEMPTS

## Recollections

Now in my seventies, I look back and puzzle how I have become an artist. I try to recall the seeds of artistic creativity scattered across the landscape of my life. Where and when did art call to me?

I recall the second-grade teacher who taught me about drawing the sky. At the window, she asked, "Where do you see the sky?"

"All over," I replied.

"Yes, the blue comes all the way down to meet the grass, doesn't it? Do you see that?"

I participated in the learning. I did not feel belittled. From then on I drew the sky all the way down to the earth, not as a blue strip across the top of my paper. I felt empowered.

I remember at age seven I scratched out a story in pencil on lined paper called "When I Was Playing with My Cousin" which began with "Ones apon a time...."

I recall the third grade when my drawing pushed against the tide of typical students' responses. I illustrated a story not with stick figures, as did everyone else. I hated drawing stick figures. Instead I drew a jelly-filled biscuit which had figured prominently in the story. The teacher raised an eyebrow but she accepted it and posted it on a board with all the others. I had resisted the norm with a different path, and was affirmed.

I recall the warm, cozy kitchen of Mrs. Graham in Bridgewater, VA, where she taught my brother and me, age ten, to draw with charcoal. How to indicate water in a glass, how to make it appear curved on flat paper. Beyond charcoal, she introduced us to colorful pastels. She praised our efforts as did our parents who smiled in approval over our artwork.

I recall when at age eleven, living with my family in Mexico, how I organized a biblical skit among neighborhood children; how I pecked out a story called "The Fairy's Secret" on Mother's Underwood typewriter, with my right arm in a cast. How I was drawn to colors — the California poppies and snapdragons growing at our doorstep, the *jacaranda* trees in the village plaza and the vibrant flower stall in the market, and above all, the colors in *serapes* and *rebozos*, worn by men and women.

I recall later times. When in high school I took Saturday drawing lessons at the county museum and when I edited the school newspaper. How I entered a short story in a Latin Forum contest in the ninth grade.

- When, in college, I squeezed in art courses among my biology labs.

- When I published my writing through the campus writing club followed by writing for the newsletter of the nursing school, and there, I wrote the history of my class for our yearbook.

- When I sewed my own clothes in college and in nursing school, crowned with helping to fashion my wedding dress and starching lace for a crown at the top of the veil.

- When I took Chinese painting lessons in Taiwan and watercolor classes in Ghana.

- When I wrote articles, poems, and devotionals for church publications, year after year.

- When I created Easter outfits for our two children, ages two and four in West Virginia, and school clothing for them and maternity clothes for myself in West Africa, having no recourse for such items in local stores.

Today I need continually to embrace the lively memories of those younger years and honor the seedlings of that time. They were significant precursors to my artistic development in later life. Some of my childhood fantasies were just fantasies, but they pointed to a creative impulse which never disappeared. In the first grade, my brother and I, along with a neighborhood friend, thought we could build a Ferris wheel with our erector set in his backyard! Wild, childish imagination audaciously sowed seeds of creativity that sprouted and matured abundantly. Picasso said, "Every child is an artist. The problem is how to remain one as he grows up."

Not envisioning an artistic goal later in life, my improvisational twists and turns while growing up silently empowered me. I seemed to have responded simply to what appealed to me at the moment, disregarding any ideas of future directions. Who would have thought that the seven-year-old and ninth grade stories would feed into my writing today? Who would have thought that my youthful art lessons and my early dressmaking attempts would prove foundational to my current fabric art? The early forays held little significance at the time, just interesting, intriguing blips and pastimes among the busyness of a life covered over with other preoccupations. Slowly, however, they grew into a compelling energy, a base of operations, as it were, with tangible proofs that art insistently remained alive. The fragments of my past became the building blocks for the future. Each fragment was reshaped for new usefulness. Even I was reshaped. The seminal interests and urges planted in earlier years remained as seeds and seedlings in a greenhouse until brought out and allowed to mature. God had a time line for them to grow and bloom when I did not. A proverb from Ghana proclaimed "God's time is best." Indeed, my becoming an artist later in life developed at just the best time.

Art making persistently knocked at my door; it never gave up on me.

Since I did not devote my life's direction to artistic attractions and interests, they lay dormant. Art was never a vocational choice. Instead, I directed my energies toward a sense of call to serve others. I strived to enter the great river of faithful people who reach out with a helping hand. I investigated careers in a medical field, teaching, and Christian education. My love of science plus the idea of medicine as ministry led me to nursing school. I envisioned doing nursing in a setting deprived of health essentials, possibly as a mission co-worker beyond our borders, such as Congo or Ecuador.

Painting and drawing took a backseat to hospital duty, attendance in labor and delivery or the operating room, sitting, observing, ambulating and medi-cating patients, taking patients' vital signs, on and on. Becoming a nurse com-pletely absorbed me. I studied hard and wanted to excel. I could only respond to God's call by doing my best

The sense of call to nursing and then to overseas service crippled the nurture of art. I viewed it merely as a hobby and a happy pastime. It never occurred to me that art had any usefulness. I did not fathom how it could communicate God's love to others. In no way could art overturn warlords and slumlords, ex-tract people from poverty and illiteracy, or make the sick well. I reasoned that the world needed more practical steps to remedy the world's ills — money, food, medical supplies and know-how shared within the framework of God's love.

In those days, I did not even perceive the connection between art and God, between art and faith, or between art and humankind's spiritual hunger. I did not fathom how art making actually could be a doorway to God.

• • •

Seeds germinate and grow when provided water, light and good soil. Likewise the seeds of creativity grow only with proper influences. These good influences — the right time, place, and energy plus encouraging family and teachers — wax and wane over the course of a lifetime. Seeds and seedlings of artistic creativity frequently suffer neglect in the frazzle of career and family life. Pressures and expectations undercut a receptive mode to the artistic spirit. Art is seen then as frivolous and non-essential in the daily mix.

Too often, I tend to shut out the light and water: "I don't have time to draw or paint." "My family comes first." "I am committed to other concerns." Many good reasons along with lame excuses tamp down the tender seeds of artistic aspirations. Art too often stagnates at the bottom of my *To Do* lists. If I truly want to create art I have to ask why I cannot seem to do so. In assessment mode, I have to seriously ask myself: "What is of ultimate importance to me? Do I continually succumb to the tyranny of the urgent? If I knew I had only a year left to live, would other priorities fly to the top of the *To Do* list?"

When my preschool children romped underfoot, they constituted the day-in-day-out priority in my life. I rarely had time of my own. Still, the urge to paint or write occasionally boiled over. I'd try to wedge artistic projects into the conglomerate of my usual bustle. Instead of a whole day devoted to sewing, I sat at my machine, twenty minutes here, thirty minutes there. I wrote when my children took naps. I painted with them. Of course by the time my three children left home, I had more time and energy. Weariness and worry lifted. I could focus on things other than their homework, allowances, driver's licenses and school grades. I was set free to fly.

## Renewed Vitality

When we moved to Ghana, West Africa, I was thirty-three years-old. My husband Pete accepted a call as Protestant chaplain at the University of Cape Coast, ninety miles west of the capital, Accra, situated on the Gulf of Guinea. In the early weeks there, with no washing machine and no hired washer-man, we washed our clothes — by hand. Pete innovatively threw clothes and linens into the bathtub, ran water and detergent on them and stomped them with his feet. Harry and Lynne, ages four and two and a half, played happily with paper, scissors, glue and crayons, which we had brought with us in our suitcases.

Other toys would arrive later in our freight and usurp the creative efforts they produced with so few materials.

In the thirteen years of slower-paced life in Africa, seeds sprouted and artistic expressions bloomed for several reasons. Our kids were in an international school. I had full-time household help and I could find no work as a foreign nurse, mainly because local nurses abounded in Ghana while in Nigeria, expatriate medical personnel and hospitals were outlawed. My dream of being a missionary nurse crumbled. I looked around for other things to do, other *worthwhile* activities I could write home about. Many of them fell apart: when people who had expressed interest to join a study group repeatedly failed to show up; when a major opportunity to teach was cut short by a siege of hepatitis which left me bedridden; when a possibility to participate with a team to address village health needs never materialized.

Un-tethered from full or part time work meant that I could use my time as I wished. Consuming projects did not cram my life. I did whatever mission work I could. I attended worship and eventually preached occasionally in a church or for vespers in secondary schools. I assisted in developing two Sunday schools. My week-day calendar harbored fewer than three engagements most weeks. Nevertheless, life overflowed with challenges. The lack of household appliances (except for a refrigerator and a stove) made housekeeping complicated. Meals were created from scratch. Clothes had to be hand washed and ironed. Tile floors were mopped daily. Because we hired a Ghanaian cook-steward to do much of this drudgery, I had a good deal of freedom. Still, shopping, searching for scarce food and household items, bargaining, planning meals with local produce and without the usual western packaged, canned or frozen foods or traditional recipes required continual adaptation. (We did without $25-dollar chickens and abandoned spaghetti when imported cheese and spices were contraband for two years.) By night time, my energy flagged in the sodden heat. I lapsed into the luxury of reading novels, literature about Africa and books on the spiritual life. I reflected. I wrote in my journal. Eventually, I re-learned to pray.

Living in Ghana also enhanced my husband's and my creativity. We had to improvise and make things we needed, or did without them. Sparsely stocked department, furniture or hardware stores compelled us to resort to our own devices. I sewed colorful striped remnants alternating with natural muslin into large squares for a king-sized bedspread. Pete engineered a filing system from emptied gallon powdered milk cans stacked on their sides in a pyramid. A dining table resulted from stained plywood mounted on cinder blocks and a desk from a refrigerator crate. Two innovative Halloween costumes spiraled from my imagination. Mosquito netting for fairy wings and an aluminum foil crown for Lynne, then a dyed mop head, a necklace of dried chicken bones, a contrived hunchback with a pillow under Dad's grey sweat suit, and watermelon rind teeth for our junior monster son. They won first prizes at school.

In the second year in Ghana, I found myself surprisingly pregnant. I felt the world closing in upon me. With no occupation in the nursing field, I decided to write a novel, something brewing in my gut for several years. In the University library, I had read many writers and books on writing. They challenged me to try writing full time. My chief misgiving, though, consisted of the fact that I, a mission co-worker would be writing a *novel*, of all things. It seemed incongruent with my call. I felt, however, that the story was important enough to tell and had ramifications for mission work in Africa. It dealt with how racial prejudice in the United States undercuts attempted outreach in Africa, told from our experience of discrimination against two men from Congo visiting us in South Carolina. I resolutely worked on it for three years, even committing myself to re-do the whole thing mid-way through all its pages. It never was published but I learned how to write and to commit myself to writing day after day, week after week.

By the fifth year in Ghana, the newness had worn off, and the creativity expressed in setting up our house had dissipated. Each day's tedium sapped my energy. My prayer life also dried up in the lethargy of tropical heat. I had nothing of faith concerns to share with others: the messenger had no message. The spiritual gauge registered empty. I became indifferent to Sunday worship, reading Scripture and prayer. A later moratorium on accepting foreign nurses led to the despairing question as to why I was in Africa at all.

Then, one day, a friend prayed with me about our forthcoming furlough. It was as if a log jam broke. Alone that night, an overwhelming visitation of God's presence flooded me. God's Spirit poured into my dry, dusty soul like a river. I felt re-created.

With the release of the Spirit a new vitality coursed through my body and soul. In my contacts with people, both planned and spontaneous, I had something to share: that God was alive, well, real and overflowing with Love. I spoke more convincingly about God in conversations with Africans and expatriate acquaintances. I also began earnestly to preach and teach, in church and seminary settings. In a land where sick and injured people's needs rose in inverse proportion to the lack of medical resources to heal them, I interceded for others, sometimes with startling results.

My artistic creativity also sprouted and grew as I experienced for the first time the connection between God's Spirit and making art. Germinated in the light and water of God's presence, artistic seeds sprouted in a resurrected vigor. They burst into all sorts of art forms. I composed songs on my autoharp and shared them with family and mission groups. I wrote poems and articles which were published in Presbyterian media back home and worked with the Christian Council of Ghana to produce literature for Ghanaian church members.

Additionally, my creative juices clamored to be expressed visually. I painted in watercolor, and made tissue paper collages. A collage of open hands receiving the symbols of fire and dove illustrated the newfound sense of Spirit's presence in my life. Beyond words, I resorted to art as a means to communicate how God was re-shaping my life. Artistic joy helped me come alive.

The Spirit's renewal critically opened the door to new directions for me. The opportunities to preach and teach plus the artistic and faith expressions which sprouted in Ghana served as seedlings for new possibilities. They pointed towards callings of artist, writer and minister, although some decades passed before they matured, flowered and then bore fruit. Decidedly, our residence in Africa brought the seeds out of the quiescent greenhouse to begin to grow steadily in the water and light of God.

## Keeping Creativity Alive

Ever since our final return to the United States, I have continued to create necessities from materials at hand, in a spontaneous improvisational manner. Doing so ignites my imagination and artistic impulses. I created front door curtains from wide semi-sheer strips of muslin which I overlapped, and curtains for other windows from my fabric stash. We made book shelves from handsome boards and cleaned-up bricks. My computer sits on the surfaces of a two-drawer file cabinet and a typing table. Instead of buying a light-weight spread for our bed for summer, I commandeered a flannel winter bed sheet to use for that purpose. We find it resourceful, money-saving and fun to put different items to different, unexpected uses.

Even for an artistic project, I squash the impulse to run out to buy what is needed. If I sit down to make art and notice paint, brushes or paper missing or in short supply, or if I can't find just the right shade of blue fabric, I tune in to my imagination. Limited resources enhance creativity, I had discovered in Africa. Instead of buying what I need, I improvise. When I put only four colors or four fabrics in front of me to create a composition, I am challenged to find ways to fully use just the supplies at hand. I create new colors, or combine existing ones in unusual ways. Many quilt guilds do just this. They initiate challenges in which members create quilts with limited, designated colors and patterns of fabrics.

Ever since our African sojourn and ever since the riveting colors of my *Passion* quilt had captured me I am magnetically drawn to color and creative possibilities, even when I am out and about, mixing and mingling. In my imagination, I consider how I can put this color with this pattern of fabric, how to mute color, how to highlight it, all during shopping or committee attending or cooking dinner. I suddenly visualize what would make an electrifying embellishment on a piece in my studio. I find surprising solutions to artistic or writing impasses away from my studio or computer when I simply open my eyes and my awareness. When I drive somewhere and muse on my writing or my art, an insight occurs on how to shift a piece of fabric in a new quilt or a paragraph in a piece of writing. Anything can trigger these responses, from scraps of wrapping paper to color combinations in a dress shop to a phrase from a speaker on the car radio.

Discovering artistic possibilities can happen any time, anywhere. Gardening, loading the dishwasher, running errands — any mundane activity may be the seedbed for fruitfulness. Albert Einstein said many of his great ideas occurred to him while he was in the shower. With or without the right mood and place, imaginative ideas sprout. I cannot control the creative impulse; I have to be tuned into it whenever it chooses to appear. Like prayer-on-the-go, I have to be open on the go to capture the new inspirations and ideas that beckon to me.

Although artistic ideas sometimes rise up impulsively, setting aside intentional time for openness and presence will enliven the seeds of creativity. Taking a time-out — as simple as taking a walk — helps to discern what to do, whether I am blocked in the middle of a project, whether I don't know how to start a new one or whether only a vague desire to create keeps surfacing. A purposeful, extended time-out helps me to fully engage my senses: such as scheduling a time to listen to nature or a chorale; inhaling fragrances in a rose garden; tasting an exotic cuisine totally foreign to me; learning to recognize the clothing in my closet simply by touch; or viewing a foreign film, pottery in a gallery and junk in a flea market. Above all, I want to feel alive in my time-out and feel delight. By doing so, I envision myself stroking the creative seeds in my greenhouse and encouraging their germination. This mini-vacation is based on a trust that vitality and freshness for a new or existing project will show up when needed. My time-out also allows for communion with God through my senses. It helps me empty out my concerns, pre-occupations, and stresses. As long as they fill up my awareness nothing else can gain entrance.

A California artist friend chooses a day of the week to go to a nearby town just to look, to relax, and to feast. She returns to her home and studio with no specific ideas for her next project. Rather, she feels intoxicated with sensory engagements, refreshed and washed with waves of wellbeing. She stores the day's sensory delights into her memory bank knowing that they will nurture her next project.

I cannot do without time-outs for visual feasting. Seven Sisters Gallery in Black Mountain has become a treasure trove of beauties to feed my soul whenever I stroll through it. The Celtic knot jewelry. The pottery in muted shades. The soft, hand-woven shawls. The comical fabric dolls. The etchings of North Carolina wild flowers. On one particular time-out I wandered through a gallery in Asheville where I encountered an exhibit of found objects fashioned into portraits of people. Faces from the lids of paint cans, eyes of electrical sockets or of stove and watch dials, noses of keys or latches, hair of rope or electrical wire, bodies of rusted metal, tarpaper or 9" x 13" baking pans. The captions matched the whimsy of the portraits: "Miss Helen is 80 years-old. She tells everybody she is 70. She says people don't need to know everything."

The imagination of this artist stirred me. I delighted in his creativity. In many time-outs I have also stumbled into some startling techniques in fiber which have set me on a new path. Like large swaths of paint across fabric, or a clever use of raw edges in a composition.

I need images to fire the image-making capacity within me, whether out-and-about or in my home, which holds many art objects for stimulation, in paper, fiber and clay. I also try to keep a notebook of arresting pictures cut from magazines and paste them down in innovative ways. As I talk on the phone in my studio, I pick up scraps of fabric lying on the table, doodle with them, and collage them in my quilt journal. All these efforts keep the seedbed of my creativity fertile and alive. They encourage and develop my visual acuity.

Art objects around me help focus my attention on reality. Pushing aside superficial concerns and invaders into my awareness, I must be reminded of who I am, that my life with God forms my center, and that I make art as a major investment. Someone has said that we need to pay attention to what we see in our household because what we see influences the direction of our lives and reaffirms our intentions. Margaret Miles tells the story of arriving in her walk-up flat in Rome after a heavy, draining day of doing research in the city. At the top of her stairs, an image of Mary and her baby adorns the wall. When she sees it, her energy is restored as she gazes on the scene. She becomes aware of God's presence in her life and her ultimate concern regarding her stay in Rome.

Some artists have noticed that their spiritual vitality enhances their creativity. Art making wells up from one's soul and expresses the longings deep inside. The Shakers declared "Hands to work, hearts to God." This, I believe, was not just an intentional effort to live in God's presence as one worked, but a living out of the reality that God and creative efforts were intertwined. Art making encourages prayer; prayer often encourages art making. The two seem to proceed in tandem.

## Seeds in a Quilt

The quilt that I named *Fertile Seeds* issued from an invitation to enter a piece into a juried book of mandala quilts. I kept a mandala journal when transitioning from writing to visual art. I kept the journal on most days of the week by filling in spontaneous shapes and colors within circles. *Fertile Seeds* was the first design in that journal, dated October 5, 1993. I made the design without deliberate thought. I drew it spontaneously, picking up colors of oil pastels I was attracted to on that particular day. With the design of fertile seeds I somehow intuited that a promising artistic prospect lay in my immediate future. The mandala in the journal proved to be a harbinger of art flourishing in my life.

Although I make most of my quilts improvisationally, *Fertile Seeds* was not one of them. It was patterned after the design in my journal. So I auditioned fabrics in the mandala colors: purples, lavenders, blues and pinks, some in solids and some in subtle prints. For a few days, I let them lie on tables and chairs in my work space while I ruminated which to select. I discarded a background of mottled batik with lavenders and pinks, and settled on a creamy drapery-like fabric with a soft sheen. It highlighted the colors in the mandala to a better advantage.

Once I decided on the fabrics for the mandala, I cut them in crescent shapes, and overlapped them to form a circle. A darker purple formed the outer crescents with the inner ones of a lighter lavender and blue with a touch of yellow. They curved over an embryo-like center with a shimmering circle of gold fabric on which I mounted a smaller hand-painted disc of bright orange and yellow. In this disc, on tiny circles of shiny red fabric, I sewed four red beads with smaller gold beads in their centers: *seeds.* Wisps of crescents spinning from the center gave a sense of motion, as if the mandala circled around in space. I sewed a few beads in the perimeter and scattered one to two-inch pieces of bright yellow embroidery floss across the quilt to add further energy. I fastened all the pieces to the background by sewing ivory colored tulle over the piece in one-inch squares.

I finished in time to have the quilt photographed and mailed. It was not juried into the book. Over 120 entries poured in, and only 80 were selected. I was not surprised. Neither was I keenly disappointed. I have treasured the quilt and was happy that the encouragement of a contest prompted me to make this keepsake which heralded my journey into art. It unequivocally declared my identity as an artist.

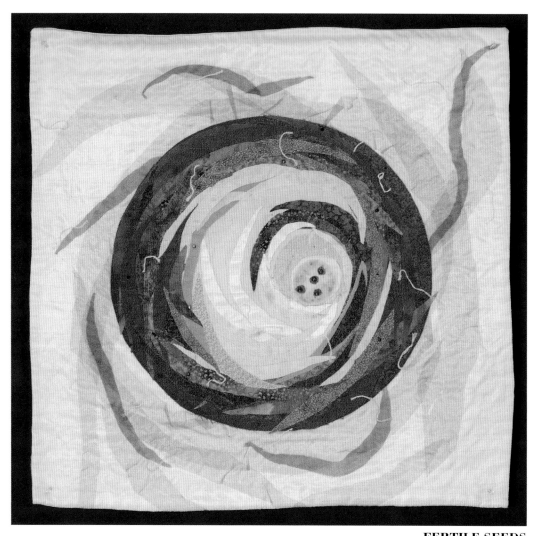

**FERTILE SEEDS**
24.5 x 25.5"

*"Germinated in the light of God's presence,
artistic seeds sprouted vigorously in many forms."*

# 8

## PAIN AND CREATIVITY: TWO RESPONSES

For four months in the winter of 2010 I endured unrelenting pain. Disks in my spine are degenerating, causing pressure on the sciatic nerve. To me, all the way down my left leg and wrapped around my ankle, sciatic pain felt like an internal barbed wire which was jerked every few minutes. Codeine derived pain killers and physical therapy with stretching exercises did little to relieve it. I could sleep only with ice packs pressed against hip, calf and ankle. I walked with a cane and secured a handicap placard for the car, both at my physician's orders. Still, I generally avoided going out if I had to walk a great distance from the car to a meeting place. Handicap parking could not be guaranteed in any given parking lot. To grocery shop, I used a motorized chair plus my husband's help to lift heavy items.

The gray, dull and biting cold of that winter, a record in the ten years of our living in North Carolina, did nothing to lift my spirits. It joined with the episodes of pain to bear down on me. A house shut against the cold plus heavy clothing and bed covers further hemmed me in. In early February I wrote in my journal, *Lord, let me not succumb to self-pity and a blue spirit. But I am tired of gray days, tired of the cold, tired of the pain, tired of poor sleep, tired of being tired!* Looking back, I was indeed depressed over constrictions and being housebound. The person I knew as Myself seemed to have vanished. I rarely related to my usual friends and associates. If any one were to ask me

"What are you working on these days?" I would have to respond, "Nothing." My answer called into question my identity. Who was I anymore?

You would think that such a quiet and alone time might be a gift. Artists and writers need solitude to work, but my cup ran over with it. *Was it a fruitful time to create with no outside distractions? Nothing to lure me away from work at hand?*

*Did I write?* No. Not even a few paragraphs a week.

*Did I play with my fabric in my studio?* No.

*Would I have found energy and excitement in the colors spilling from my cupboards?* Certainly, but not now.

*Would scattering fabric scraps around in my studio so I could keep them in my sight, and even doodling with them not lift my spirits?* No.

*So, I didn't do any of these things?* No.

*Did I spend extended times in prayer in an imposed private retreat?* No. I believed that God companions us in our distresses and suffers when we suffer. God was with me, but I was not responding to God's presence. I was too self-absorbed with my constant pain.

*Did I journal?* Only to lament to God.

*Did I read uplifting spiritual books?* Sometimes.

*Did I read other things?* Yes, a lot. I tried going through some books in order to downsize my collection. I read from Susan Howatch, British novelist; from Peter Tremayne, writer of things Celtic. I read Sarah Lawrence Lightfoot's book, *The Third Chapter: Passion, Risk, and Adventure in the 25 Years after 50*; and re-read Mary Catherine Bateson's *Composing a Life*. I read Kingsolver's new book *The Lacuna*, and on the sofa at night I plowed through Erskine Clarke's 500-page *Dwelling Place — A Plantation Epic*, about slavery in Coastal Georgia in the 1800's. I dipped into other books lying on my shelf, rejected them and eventually gave them away.

*Did I exercise or stretch?* Yes, everyday, with forced determination. I also walked and dangled in the local swimming pool.

*Did I preach?* I managed, three times.

*Did I keep house?* No. Between my twice-a-month cleaning woman and supportive husband, they kept things cleaned and us fed. I lolled in a comfortable chair, my cane at my side, noticing things that needed attention but letting them go: spots on the kitchen floor or the carpet, overflowing waste baskets, magazines in disarray. I began to see myself as a compulsive tidy-upper.

In my journal, I asked numerous "what if's."

*What if I don't get over this?*
*What if I spend the rest of my days in pain with great limitations?*
*What if I lived alone without Pete's support?*
I also wrote
*Don't lament limitations and loss; instead celebrate what you do have!*
And
*Help me accept this empty, uncreative time.*

I found solace in worship when I was able to attend, especially at St. James Episcopal Church which sponsored a healing service every Wednesday. At home, I had difficulty sitting for any length of time to pray, but Scripture buoyed me up and kept me from drowning. I recalled the amazing verses from *Habakkuk Four* where the prophet cries in extremis: "Though the fig tree does not blossom, and no fruit is on the vines; though the produce of the olive fail and the fields yield no food; though the flock is cut off from the fold and there is no herd in the stalls, yet I will rejoice in the Lord; I will exult in the God of my salvation." I had discovered the verses in Ghana after I had run our Peugeot station wagon into a concrete, three-foot gutter at the roadside. The wheels on the right side of the car were ruined. Ghana had no replacements at the time. I sat alone in the dark that night, lamenting and pouring over these verses. With great effort, I tried to "rejoice" in God in spite of the circumstances, trying to believe that the problem would be resolved in due course.

Slowly, it was, but we had to be car-less for three days. Now, remembering these verses from long ago, I took heart and pleaded for patience.

I leaned into God's promise of Isaiah 58:9, "...you shall call, and the Lord will answer; you shall cry for help, and he will say, 'Here I am'."

Why was it "an *uncreative* time?" What was going on?

During this time, my artist friend, Mary Logan, suffered with temporomandibular disorder, (TMJ), an acutely painful disorder in the face. She found it very difficult to chew food, and even to talk. We discussed the affects of pain on one's creativity. She said that pain sapped all her energy. With that disappearing plus the assault on her identity as an artist melting away, she became depressed. "Will I ever create again?" she wondered.

I found myself in similar straits.

Eventually, I received an epidural injection of cortisone into my spine in late March. It usually takes three injections, a week apart, to relieve the pain, but mine was relieved with only one. Life began again. My energy was restored, my outlook brightened, my creativity surged. My doctor's nurse said, "You must be thanking God a dozen times a day!"

Absolutely.

■ ■ ■

Pain can take many forms with many levels of severity, and occasional outbursts of relief. It can visit us physically, emotionally, mentally and/or spiritually. About ten years previously a situation of pain attacked me in the form of emotional turmoil. Interestingly, I had the energy this time to try to resolve what it was doing to me. Anger was the source of my pain, and I intuitively knew that it could destroy me. Clarissa Pinkola Estes confirms my realization when she speaks of the need to confront anger, otherwise it's "like putting fire into a burlap bag." She says that sometimes women use rage to empower themselves. Care must be taken, however, because ongoing rage "is a fire that burns [one's] primary energy."

I was angry because my husband was working himself to death. Pete was Executive Director of a church-sponsored 33-bedroom guest house, Villa International Atlanta, for international medical personnel. As Director, he assumed the role of raising more than one million dollars to expand the house. To do this, he had to stimulate support from churches and ecclesiastical bodies all over Georgia, South Carolina and Florida.

Although he did not work on a commission basis, nor was his salary docked if he did not bring in a quota of funds, he drove himself mercilessly. No one could fault him for a lack of commitment or doing a half-baked job. He was extremely conscientious, with a farmer's mentality of doing whatever needed to be done, from pre-dawn to post-dusk. He endured long road trips so he could meet with people en route to his next speaking engagement. I literally thought he would die, especially on his many business ventures. He would drive 450 miles to Orlando, Florida from our Atlanta home for a one-night meeting and then drive back the same distance the next day, stopping off to visit pastors and church boards along the way. Then he would hold meetings as soon as he returned, followed by another lengthy trip right after that. Although exhaustion enfolded him like a wool blanket, he refused to take time off. He was too tired to get out of his chair to go and get a report. He was too tired to load his car for the next trip. "I work the job, not the hours," he said. His closest friend told him he would never retire: "They will carry you out of here, feet first."

I became frantic with his behavior. I wrote about it in my journal, *Exhaustion. Sleepless nights, total absorption in your work, overwhelmed by it so you don't have a life of your own.* I feared his not ever coming back home, his falling asleep at the wheel, even his making a devastating mistake at a board meeting or a church function because of fatigue. One time he drove most of the pre-dawn hours from one town to another to address a meeting. There, to a group of women, he said that the previous night he had "slept with Margaret." He had intended to say that he had slept in her home as her and her husband's guest. He was unaware of his blooper until someone pointed it out to him.

Occasionally I pounded him with critical questions. "Can't you ever call in sick or take a day off? Can't you ask someone else to do some of this promotional effort? You say, 'I can't do it all,' then what follows from that? You still try to do it all as far as I can see. Can't you leave some things undone, or delegate? Where will it all end except in an early death or else physical collapse leading to incapacity?" I would call the roll of complaints. I felt like a worn out broken record, one which he had learned simply to turn off. Worry wracked me with insomnia. Fear stalked me at night. Anger gripped me, stifled me and rendered me totally helpless.

I considered how I should act around him: *Do I mirror his tiredness? Do I speak back to him the craziness of his life? Do I show compassion if I can even summon it?*

I considered his work as his other wife while I faded from view. Am I needed here?

I wondered whether to stay or to leave. But, no. Leaving was not an option I would entertain. I was committed to him and to our marriage, for better or worse. Furthermore, I felt it would be more stressful for me to leave than to stay. I needed to stay put with serenity somehow and to *defect in place*, a phrase I had overheard, possibly from disenchanted wives.

I also pondered, *What in the world would I do, left here as a widow? Where would I go? I can't stay in this apartment. Would I remain in Atlanta? Try to pastor a church? Move closer to one of our three children?*

I made sure his life insurance topped out at the highest level.

We lived in a spacious apartment in the guesthouse. With our living where Pete worked, it meant he affixed himself to his work like fleas on a dog. "Living in" also meant we were forever on call. Although the co-director alternated with us to take calls, intrusions still badgered us at all hours. Since Pete either plied the interstates or collapsed on the bed at an early hour, I frequently fielded the interruptions. I answered the door, showed new guests to their room (even after midnight), and still later helped find what they needed, sold stamps, showed how to make long distance calls to China or Kenya or wherever, demonstrated how to use equipment in the kitchen, how the building was locked up at night, how to catch the city bus, on and on. The guest house paid me modestly for my efforts during a few years prior to retirement.

At the same time, I interacted with my mother who had recently moved into a nearby retirement home. Her memory began to teeter between clarity and fog. I had to relieve her of her checkbook, whereupon she lashed out at me in anger. "I've been a bookkeeper all my life, for heaven's sake!" she fumed at me more than once.

In 2000 we left the guest house and retired in our own home, in a small, quiet town surrounded by North Carolina mountains. The contrast staggers me as I reflect on our former life. I don't know how I endured our 18 years in that situation. Only now have I realized the extensive pain and continual stress that enveloped me while coping with the guest house, my husband and my mother. Friends used to ask me how I tolerated it all. I would shrug and say, "I get by." I recall how I barely managed, and how often I lashed out at the dysfunction in judgment and anger. A few years ago, at a retreat, I found myself describing my life in the guest house with the person next to me. She asked incredulously, "How did you do it?" My non-thinking immediate reply came: "I became a contemplative."

Retreating to God had become urgent. I got up before anyone else, before the staff opened the offices, before guests interrupted, and I embraced silence. When the new chapel was built, it became my hallowed ground, my safe haven in dawn's golden light. I had designed the chapel. Everything in it succored me. The mauves and aquas in the chairs and cushions, the candles, the plants, the fabric wall hanging I had created, the framed prints of international interpretations of Christ's face, the glass doors opening to the woods. With a lit candle flickering before me, I sat on a floor cushion and gazed outside. In the spring, a honeysuckle vine wrapped around a nearby tree and formed a nest for cooing doves. Their soft notes comforted my bruised spirit.

•••

Something needed to change, but I certainly could not change my place of living nor could I change Pete's behavior or my mother's slow slide to oblivion. Too often I would try to get around his work fixation by making plans for fun. His co-director once gave him a year's calendar with recreational options marked on it. She, too, saw the over-work. I also tried calendar arrangements but to no avail. One wedding anniversary we agreed to go to Lake Lanier for fun. It never happened. Arranging space in his new office and making new file folders won out while I tried to find something else to do. I simmered and burned.

I became aware of how judgmental I had become, not only towards the domestic issues at hand, but with everyone and everything else as well. I always second-guessed people. My criticisms lay silently in wait like a trap which sprang on unsuspecting victims if they didn't measure up to my standards. Their appearance, their actions, their words, their motivations all fell under the scrutiny of my evaluation of them.

The judge in me turned its gaze back on me. I then reached one difficult conclusion: *I could only change myself.* I had to let go of my expectations. I had to relinquish my resentment over imperfect behaviors and a demanding environment. Shifting judgment to me for a change, I simply viewed myself as unforgiving, angry and critical. As best I could, I tried dealing with these attributes. I sought a diminishment in their stranglehold on me. I participated in group therapy for two years. I also attended a few Al-Anon meetings thinking the participants there really knew how to handle anger, criticalness and addiction. Neither group fully met my needs.

I wrote in my journal:

> *I cannot change him.*
> *I can only change myself.*

*I cannot change myself*
*Except by your power, O God.*
*Heal me, Lord, and I shall be healed.*
*I cannot love;*
*I cannot forgive*
*Only you can*
*In me, through me and in spite of me.*

I didn't know where to turn. I felt a sense of rightness when, with no fore-thought, an opportunity presented itself. My thoughts randomly settled on a book in my collection, *Coming Home: A Manual for Spiritual Direction.* An exercise in it spoke to me: "A Quality I Would Like to Say Goodbye To." Im-mediately, I put "criticalness" in the cross-hairs. I wrote, *This quality is the Judge in my life. The one who knows how to do things better than anybody else, from preaching to cleaning up the kitchen. It always suggests a better way, and simply cannot resist verbalizing it.... No one can measure up to how to do things right.... I am beginning to wonder if I can ever relate to people in a non-judging fashion....* The book suggested an exercise in "active imagina-tion." Done consciously and wide awake (as opposed to dreaming), such a process can offer resolution and change.

In a comfortable chair, I sat in a relaxed pose, and gave permission to whatev-er might arise. Right away a figure appeared in my imagination whom I called Juris, the judge. He was a masculine figure, suggesting an aggressive style. He wore a black robe — the same thing that ministers of my denomination wear as we lead worship. The similarity unnerved me. His stringy grey hair hung down to his collar. Juris had a hooked nose (for prying) and thick eyeglasses (the better to scrutinize faults). He had long bony fingers (good for pointing out imperfections) and a very sour, disagreeable demeanor. His penetrating eyes looked over his glasses at me condescendingly as he sat behind his im-posing high bench and desktop which put distance between him and me.

We sparred with words back and forth for awhile. I told him that I wanted to get to know him since he so dominated my life. At first he resisted the intrusion but I persisted in my desire to get acquainted. I told him my need to reduce the judging aspect of my life.

Then he declared "Wherever there is a vacuum, it is filled. A law of nature, which I am sure you know." Sarcasm tinged his voice as he glared at me.

"What do you mean?"

"I, the Judge, arose to power out of default. I grasped my position in you because another power or person was not allowed to. She wasn't strong enough." he responded.

"Strong enough?"

"There is a part of you that is poorly developed. It has become stunted. And that part is caring. And creating."

"What has happened to stunt her growth?" I asked.

He said that I had not given enough time to creativity. "You are analytical. It serves you well, most of the time" he said, "but turn your analysis to things, not people. Turn your judging towards words and sentences and characterization, and how to say things. Turn it towards shape and color and shading instead of others' flaws. In this way, you will be able to discern in people not their faults, but their needs. From that, your compassion will grow, and so will your creativity."

He warned me not to banish Juris, but to channel him positively. "I'm not Judas, but an ally if you respect me."

*So that's what judging is for*, I mused and felt elated that a loathsome characteristic could be transformed. I would plunge into the writing I was engaged in at the time, not only to communicate well but to bring healing to myself.

I needed to find a symbol representing my renewed commitment to write and decided on a feather: a natural ancient implement for writing. It would remind me that I needed judgment in my efforts to write, that criticalness had its good purposes. I would be encouraged that my judging others, notably

Pete, would shrink.

I found the feather where I expected: the gathering spot of pigeons in the outside corner of my Seminary's library. I collected the silver-grey feather, ran my fingers along its shaft, and took it home. It enabled me to smile as I sifted through my writing, judging what belonged and what did not, what needed changing and what could remain undisturbed.

Later, I connected with Juris when I wrote a book for my Church describing the work of Presbyterian churches in ten African countries. When I visited them, I had stayed in each country only a few days. I supplemented the on-site material with interviews of Africans in Atlanta along with Americans who had lived in Africa. Books and periodicals in my college library helped fill in the gaps. I feared that my book, called *God's Fire*, would appear extremely superficial and naïve. My efforts were supremely rewarded, however, when a Kenyan in Atlanta congratulated me for clearly describing the life of the African church and its people.

I could not have written the book without Juris at my side. In the mix of count-less interviews, visits to church ministries, numberless meetings and worship services I attended, no way could I have discerned what to include and what to discard. I had unconsciously called on Juris in every situation to help me judge the importance of each bit of information, and then to weave my notes and scribbles into an effective whole.

A few years later, I would use Juris to determine which fabrics to use, how to arrange them and become a fabric artist.

■ ■ ■

Embracing Juris did not cure my critical nature all at once. I struggled to turn off judging others. I looked for other helps and recalled a published article of mine, *St Thérèse and I, and the Struggle to Love.* It described my dilemma. Originally, I regarded St. Thérèse of Lisieux as a syrupy saint. Years before, in my college's library stacks, I had read pieces of her autobiography with its lavish, flowery language which jangled my sensibilities. I had quickly snapped the book shut. It fairly offended me. But thirty-five years later in a seminary class, her name and her work arrested my attention. She really knew how to love others — the disagreeable others around her — and to pour out tender compassion and care.

Once more, I took up her autobiography, *Story of a Soul*. I tenaciously plowed through her effusive self-expression to unearth the kernel of truth. I discovered that she felt her vocation was to love. Such love was expressed in the symbol of scattering petals of flowers for Jesus — doing little actions of self-sacrifice. Assisting a crippled nun to meals, washing extra clothing in the laundry, listening attentively to boring tales. She called it her "little way," which has attracted ordinary people in our day and age to follow her path. She may have called it "little," I call it "tough."

With fierce determination I tried following her example. I gritted my teeth to be more loving. I managed to hold my tongue a little more patiently. But slippery criticisms wormed their way into my thoughts. Towards Pete: *Why can't he see he's killing himself?* And towards others: *Why does she always have to put herself down? Won't he ever get a grip on his overeating? Seems like I've heard this before — a hundred times.* On and on streamed the inner critique of persons around me.

Apparently St. Thérèse had a hard time loving, too. She complained that she could never hope to love the sisters in her convent the way Jesus did. She asked him to love them through her. "I know that when I am charitable, it is Jesus acting through me, and that the more closely I unite myself to Him, the more I will be able to love all my sisters."

Her words spoke to me. To grow in charity and acceptance, would require "unit[ing] myself to him." But how? I began to pray in silent attentiveness, something new to me. No words, just presence. I had to let go of many thoughts and agendas as I prayed. Becoming empty before God, I had to drop plans for today and the remembrance of mistakes from yesterday. Praying this way proved to be very hard. My thoughts invariably slipped into other concerns. Additionally, I found it simply hard to sit still for ten to twenty minutes trying not to ruminate. I soon discovered that the letting go seeped out to other concerns. I was slowly relinquishing my expectations of people. Detachment from words in prayer evolved along with detachment from negative assessments of people.

This Protestant began to call on St. Thérèse for help. She had said she would spend her heaven doing good on earth and praying for people. So I called on her as I would phone a friend to pray with me. I imagined her at times sitting opposite me in her brown habit and her shy smile, very self-effacing, very young.

St. Thérèse and Juris: what a pair! The insights gained from the two intertwined so I could take steps toward compassion: through contemplative prayer and through creativity. Through concentrated wordless prayer — and also through creative efforts — I could let go of judging people. My criticisms of others had a chance of fading away. Through art and writing, judging would be positively used in discerning words and colors. Perhaps *judging* is not the correct word to describe art making. *Discrimination*—deciding what fits or belongs, or not — says it better.

●●●

Upon encountering Juris and St. Thérèse and going deeper in self-examination, I began to discover that judging and criticalness represented mere sparks of a larger fire. At rock bottom smoldered anger. A veneer of serenity usually overlay my demeanor. People spoke of me as a calming presence. Perhaps they would have been startled to hear me confess my anger. But it was there as seen in my reaction to Pete's overwork.

I began to see that anger had its roots in my youth. During adolescence, when I began discerning what vocation to follow, I wanted to change the world. I rebelled against society's values and oppressiveness. Anger inevitably lies behind rebellion and it did mine. I was angry that the world suffered from abuse, and its inhabitants acted indifferently to its predicaments. Angry people say No to adverse conditions around them, and join others to remedy the flaws of earth. I resolved to engage the poverty, sickness, and unbelief that I perceived. By age 16, I declared to my parents that I wanted to be a nurse and a missionary. Both possibilities greatly unsettled them. They saw me as a refined socialite. I would have none of it. I revolted against their expectations for me. My dad, a civil engineer, said, "I can see going overseas and building a dam or a road. But doing something religious is beyond me." I replied, "But which is more important?" He only shook his head in incomprehension.

I had a hard time living with those immediately around me, and I'm sure they with me. They saw me as an idealistic person whose beliefs did not match their views of society. I viewed their non-understanding as indifference and uncaring. Some of my loved ones acted out in negative behaviors. Some did not support my becoming a missionary, and later, a minister. My creative path in art puzzled them. Some constantly invaded my space and suggested "better things" to do. Moreover, I turned my anger towards those — like Pete — whose lifestyles were destroying them. They would die if they didn't change their behaviors, I observed, and I found no way to intervene. I began to feel as if I harbored an angry sword in my gut toward their malignant behavior.

With startling clarity, I realized one day that that sword could kill me if I did not divert it or eliminate it. As a result I developed a visual image that evacuated the anger at hand. I imaged a four-inch metal disc edged with vicious teeth lodged in my middle. I consciously, imaginatively reached in and with a movement of my arm, flung it up into space where it could spin innocuously. I tried this every time I felt unusually stressed. The anger dissipated until the next provocation, whereupon I would throw the disc again.

Visual imaging had more power, I discovered, than wailing over inabilities. It had more power than reasoning things out, resorting to words, or fervently wishing for change. It had an immediate, therapeutic effect because I instantly felt a resolution. I believed that God's grace guided me to imagine this empowering exercise. It was another imaging resource to store for future use.

Other moments of grace came when I attended several sacred art retreats at a convent in south Florida led by Elizabeth Rosson, an art therapist and spiritual director. Upon noticing an ad about the first upcoming retreat, a friend of mine in Orlando called me and said "This has your name on it!" The retreat allowed us to "expand our experience of God through the language of art." For several unfettered days, I dived into exercises with watercolors, feeling the ecstasy of art making. I particularly reveled in painting four images of the stages of my life with a new medium, watercolor crayons. The fourth image, representing my age of 60 at the time, burst into a pulsating flower of yellow and orange on a purple and blue background. It pictured coming into full flower in my older years, alive and vibrant.

In one exercise we painted an image in a mandala. Wanting to deal with my anger issue, I picked blue, purple, red and orange. Within the swirls of blue on my paper, I painted red and purple bleeding heart flowers. Around them, I painted a circle of orange with jagged teeth. As we were directed, I placed the painting into a structure of two 12-inch square mirrors taped together at right angles. I gasped at the results. The orange teeth became de-fanged, and guarded the flowers, which were multiplied three and four times. I wrote its message to me: *Keep working on releasing your anger and befriend it. Soon it will make the flowers of your creativity expand. And note that the purple and red don't always symbolize anger, but rather energy and creative passion.*

At a later retreat, Elizabeth directed us in making a papier-mâché image of "our inner beast." I knew exactly what I needed to represent.

I had never worked with papier-mâché before. We cut strips of newspaper, wet them with wallpaper glue and covered a balloon for the head. On it, I attached short curved pieces of wire to look like hair standing on end which I painted cadmium red. The figure had a sharp nose and a gaping open mouth into which I inserted fearsome cardboard teeth. Above the flaming red cheeks, the eyebrows slanted upward over the blue eyes creating a scowl. I affixed the ears to the head and the head to the body with a hot glue gun. I seated the figure with its arms hanging down and its feet straight out in front. I created a red striped shirt and a blue vest with the emblem of a lightning bolt on it. I rolled small pieces of cardboard to make fingers, and bent and glued them painstakingly to make clenched fists. The figure sat about three feet high.

My created monster personified rage. I named him Jimmy, because James means "son of thunder." Among the group of twenty or so other creations in the class no other approximated Jimmy's ferocity. Curiously, I began to warm towards him. I wrote, *By supper time I felt a real tenderness toward this angry child who needs love.* There was something healing in seeing rage symbolically personified and sitting on a table. Jimmy had objectified my anger as I definitively pulled it out of me. At the same time, I needed to embrace Jimmy, for the anger personified in him had intertwined with judging, and my creative efforts relied on judging. But how would anger/judging and creative longings come together visually? I was still unclear how this would happen or reveal itself. The answer came through a painting I made at the retreat.

Elizabeth said, "After becoming acquainted with our inner beast we will become more acquainted with the positive inner voice in each of us — the voice of God. We call this 'The Messenger.' Express this using any materials present." I took a long walk to ponder possibilities. After awhile, I saw the image of fire. It represented an underlying anger to set things right in a chaotic world. It represented my judgmental anger towards others. But now, I saw it in a new light.

An image took shape as I painted a circular mandala. I stroked the paper with indigo blue and orange-red. With astonishment, I realized that these were the same colors I used to paint Jimmy: my colors of anger. I held my brush in mid-air questioning what was unfolding before me. For now, the image of fire emerging on my paper was not the fire of anger, but the Holy Spirit who consistently stoked my creativity, the fire that sparked every living thing as Hildegarde of Bingen had said. I believed the fiery Spirit could also tamp down my anger so judging might be defined as *discrimination*. This ability would enable me to determine what mattered, and what to include or discard in both writing and art making.

I knew now that I decidedly needed Juris as an ally; I could not banish him and remain creative. I also viewed Jimmy not as my inner beast, but rather as a dark side of me, one I needed to befriend. I brought Jimmy home with me and placed him on a shelf. Every now and then I take him down and embrace him.

## The Two Kinds of Pain

I have delved deeply into the mystery of pain in my life and how I responded so differently to the two episodes I have described. In the more recent incidence of sciatica, energy for creative efforts sank under an intense seeking diminishment of severe physical pain. As I ponder the dark time now, I see that depression may have also enveloped and depleted me. Without creative energy, artistic expression simply exited my life. My friend Connie told me not to be so worried about my inertia. "You did the best you could." So, for a time, I let go of the why's and why not's.

In the older issue of emotional pain, I actively pursued imagination, creative exercises and art to help relinquish the pain-induced criticalness and anger. I felt that if I did not find a remedy, the fire of anger would consume me and burn everyone else around me. Indeed others felt my pain also in reacting to my fiery moods.

The art retreats offered me revelation and discovery. The encounters with Juris, St. Thérèse, the whirling disc and Jimmy gifted me with insight about my emotional pain. They all invited me into the world of imagination and art making in which Spirit began to transform my negative energies into positive ones. Instead of judging others and myself, I judged my work instead. In my studio or at the computer I could shut the door on my tense and conflicted world. Serenity washed over me whenever I focused on my creative attempts. Art making has enabled me to endure.

I examined other artists. Vincent Van Gogh painted out of the pain of rejection. Frieda Kahlo objectified her multiple injuries and her failed marriage to Diego Rivera by painting them and her deep sadness on canvas. Pain stimulated her need to paint. Persons in my immediate environment have painted through their cancer and mental illness. The ones we don't hear about perhaps isolated themselves in a cave of depression and smothered feelings.

I wonder which path I will walk the next time pain invades my life. Will my writing and my art help me get through pain, or will creative efforts shut down? I doubt that I can pre-plan the best course to negotiate pain. I will simply feel my way as choices present themselves and find my path through improvisation: by doing what feels right at the time.

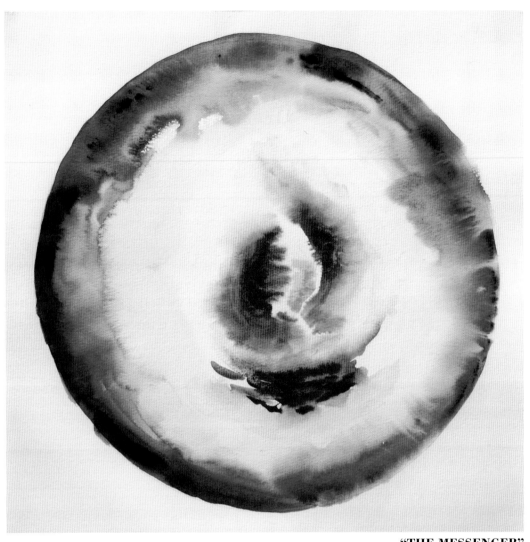

**"THE MESSENGER"**
Watercolor
15" x 15"

*"The colors in my watercolor*
*did not represent anger as before,*
*but the Spirit's fire who stokes my creativity."*

# 9

## RESISTANCE IN ART AND LIFE

In August of 2001 I visited the annual Asheville Quilt Guild show. I wandered through myriads of traditional quilts, some complex and brilliantly executed. Large ones intimidated me as I pondered how long it must have taken the quilter to hand-stitch a project. In the maze of Nine-Patches, Trips around the World, and Log Cabins, I found a few art quilts, and of these, two pulsated from black backgrounds. One of embroidered flowers in green, red and cream on black squares, and one of colorful circles attached to black particularly enchanted me. They made a bold, dramatic statement. The viewer cannot help noticing them.

### Hesitations and Fears

I resolved to use black as I began a new quilt. Deciding on black was at least a beginning. But how would I use it — as part of the surface or as the background? And what other colors would I incorporate into the black?

I entered my studio, and opened the door to my cabinet containing baskets of fabrics. Their colors streamed out to me in a life-giving flood. The blues, aquas and greens sat on one shelf, the yellows, oranges and reds resonated with each other on another. Other shelves held shades of green, purples, browns and grays. Every time I falter and wonder what to compose next, all I have to do is to glance at the fabrics in my studio. Every time their colors pull me to their bosom. Today I also heard them whispering in my ear. They insisted, *yes, you have endless ideas within you. Why not come and play with us?*

So I began. Trying to view my first steps toward a new creation as play, I pulled out a lustrous black wool along with fuchsia prints, and a tie-dye piece from Ghana in gold, tan and hot pink. Two months earlier I had attended a workshop in surface design, which led me to splashing hot pink and aqua paint on cotton fabric. I now stamped that fabric with a pearl-white grid using the bottom of a re-cycled plastic strawberry container. After finalizing these fabric selections, I tried arranging the pieces on the design wall of my studio.

The designing challenged me. I pressed a fuchsia and aqua print to the wall followed by other pieces on it. I cut strips from the black wool and then frayed the edges. I laid them in various patterns across the surface but they seemed too harsh. I eliminated them. What a waste, I sighed as I put the pieces in a plastic bag, hoping to find use for them again some other time. At that point I then decided to use the wool as the entire background.

I arranged squares and rectangles of the other fabrics on top in a diagonal affect. It had no zing.

I placed pieces in a symmetrical design with a large vertical rectangle down the middle and smaller configurations on each side. *Too pat, too simplistic, too tame*, I decided. Besides, I prefer an asymmetrical composition embedded with hidden surprises.

I still found no sense of direction. On top of the wool, I arranged and re-arranged and re-arranged. I made feeble efforts in design, placing a piece here, a piece there, re-positioning them, removing some, adding others. I intentionally kept trying possible designs and tried not to sort out solutions in my mind only. I even made sketches of each arrangement, thinking I might return to one that pleased me, but to no avail.

The piece resisted coming together. After a day or two, I walked out. I was at a loss and didn't know what to do. *I'll let it incubate*, I reasoned. I didn't know how to fix the problem or even how to name it. I was clueless and helpless. I could not move forward.

The embryo quilt hung on my studio wall for weeks, embarrassing me, imposing a great feeling of failure. I dug down deep for ideas and found none. Had the well run dry after all? Occasionally I entered my studio and stirred up courage to look at what I considered the failure on the wall, hoping that some flash of insight would come. When nothing emerged, I shook my head. I searched for more solutions in vain. So I busied myself with other things to do. I cleaned the tables, I re-arranged thread, I dusted containers of scraps, clips, and markers.

A friend who saw it said, "The pieces need to overlap."  I agreed: they certainly do.

Later, another friend said, "Make sure each piece is exposed to the black. It's the black that makes it so different, so dramatic. And I think they need to tilt against each other." I followed through on her suggestions. But I could go no further.

My quilt was resisting me, and I was resisting it.

On September 11, 2001 after 2792 died in New York City, Pennsylvania and Virginia, my quilt exploded with new life. The pieces I had printed with grids begin to look like structures built of blocks. They tumbled on the black background, with flame-shaped tie-dye showing through in reverse appliqué. In the piece I perceived buildings falling down, with flames licking the wreckage. No longer embryonic, the quilt leaped forth like a willful child with a mind of its own. I caught up with its energy and found momentum. I added fuchsia and aqua cording, and quilted the piece by tying it with bright embroidery threads. The composition then throbbed with life. It depicted 9/11, not Pentecost as I had originally thought. At first the colors seemed too joyful but after much pondering, I understood. Hope lives on even in the midst of tragedy. I named the quilt *Dance in the Darkness*.

■ ■ ■

I have confronted resistance at every level of art making, beginning at the beginning. Many potentially creative persons balk at even starting a creative project. They resist engaging in one because of inner voices of criticism left over from childhood. *You can't draw a straight line. You can't spell. You can't carry a tune.* How amazing and how sad that we can be held captive by these voices of 20, 30, 50 years ago. We live falsely by those negative assessments of our abilities, are chained by them, and in many instances, can hardly break free. Fortunately, I cannot recall any crippling judgments branded in my psyche by parents, teachers or peers. Criticisms from others, past or present, have not blocked my attempts in fabric art. Yet, something makes me hesitate when I enter my studio. In spite of my love of color and fabric, I stop at my work table, and fiddle. I get in the clean-up mode. Am I priming the pump to begin a new artistic venture, or just stalling? Something holds me back. I feel like a beginner all over again. I feel uneasy, not sure what about. I hope my unease will not take my desire to create by the throat and choke it.

Whenever hesitations clog my attempts to start a new quilt I try to analyze why. I peel back possible clues like an onion. At the core of my peeling back I discover glimpses of fear. *What am I afraid of?* I ask myself. Admission comes uneasily. Recognizing truth throws up its own barriers of resistance.

Improvisational quilt making creates innumerable resistances and fears. Unlike traditional quilts with nailed-down patterns from a book, there are no set designs, boundaries or instructions. The sky is the limit. Any juxtaposition of colors, any arrangement of design, any manner of construction is infinitely possible. The lack of limitations raises the awesome question: where to go with this project? Where does it begin and where does it end? The path to its end confronts me with a fear of the unknown.

Fear has blocked my initial creative attempts in the past. Not knowing the end result of a project or how it will be received by others has gripped me. I enter the unknowns in my life with trepidation. Instead, I want to be in control and to know outcomes, or at least if I am going in the right direction toward a destination.

I finally admit that I recognize this rather familiar fear lurking in the corners of my creative desires. Upon bringing this realization to light, limp like an airless balloon, I attempt to let go of control and fear until, depleted, I pray *This is your work. God, come to my assistance; Lord, make haste to help me.*

Can I trust that God's creating Spirit who brooded over the primordial chaos in Genesis One and brought life out of it will also enliven me?

As I stand at my studio work table before I begin, I wrestle with my fear and try to tamp it down. Surrendering to the creativity that God has planted within me, I know it will take me where I need to go. It will sustain me — even through tortuous twists and turns — to a pleasing end result. I try not to contemplate an end result. I remind myself: this is why I love improvisational quilt making. The pattern unfolds a step at a time. One thing leads to another in the mystery of proceeding to a satisfactory conclusion. The unclear path ahead amazingly offers delight which outstrips any anxiety over not knowing. I find joy and meaning in the process as much as the product, which has appeared almost magically, every time. So I move forward.

## Choosing Fabrics

In the beginning, the unborn quilt doesn't even reside in my imagination since I can visualize nothing. It resides only in my longing to make tangible something invisible, and my longing to engage in color. Frequently I have no idea which fabrics to target. *Which* fabrics, what to do with them, and *how* to start glare at me. I enter the frightening chaos of uncertainty.

The inkling of a quilt usually comes to me through a color or combination of colors, like black which initiated *Dance in the Darkness*. Certainly, the love of exuberant fabric colors enliven me. I can pull out combinations of fabric pieces from my cupboards and drawers, and fall in love with any of them. Finding enchantment everywhere I look, I can drown in possibilities. Simply adoring colors and patterns, though, will make little progress. I have to decide. Making specific choices eliminates other beautiful options. I have to choose irrevocably: this is what I want to work with, and not that.

Because I knew I wanted to include black in *Dance in the Darkness*, that one choice acted as an anchor in a sea of instability. It gave me a starting place. Most of the other quilts pictured in this book began with a choice of colors in my mind's eye. But if color choice remains fluid for too long a period, and I am flooded with options, anxiety arises. I may feel lost with no sense of direction. I may begin to resist working with this idea, this set of colors, this quilt. *This is too hard, too confusing, too nebulous,* I moan inwardly. I make myself stay in the work space to continue weighing options. Otherwise I may leave and take a needed time out to let the matter incubate.

I begin by arranging certain fabric colors together. I place those for possible inclusion all around my studio to audition them. For me, it's like playing. I experiment with certain color combinations to discern which fabrics I want to incorporate into the quilt. This step may take half a day, or more than a week, as I try various arrangements. Usually making a firm decision concerning fabrics at the beginning of a new quilt is the easiest, least anxiety-ridden aspect of the new work.

## Designing

When I finally choose the needed fabrics, I enter the design stage, an even more arduous stage. A lot of trial and error accompanies the designing process as I have indicated in working with *Dance in the Darkness.* Everything is in flux. I must try different approaches, many of which will not work. Over and over, I have to back track and begin anew. If this happens too often, I begin to resist the project. Bafflement threatens to overtake me to the point I may threaten to abandon the rudimentary quilt. The uncertainty calls into question once more my ability to create something new out of a seemingly empty imagination. I take a deep breath, stop and listen, wait and discern. Often, when I back off and take a time-out, solutions will surface and startle me. Although I have occasionally delayed finishing a difficult quilt, I haven't walked away from one without completing it. I thank an inner stamina for helping me to resist resistance.

I have told myself repeatedly, yet not followed through, that I should work at more than one quilt at a time. When I am stuck in one I could turn to another. Many artists find this a satisfactory way to work. If I adopt this pattern of working I am concerned that I will forsake the former project in favor of the latter, never complete the one I started and will end up with scores of unfinished quilts. I have to see a quilt through to the end before I begin another, lest ideas for another quilt lure me away. My love of fabrics and colors certainly could sabotage a present effort and easily steer me toward beginning another quilt.

Many future directions beckon me. In my imagination resides a stash of quilt projects that I hope to attempt some day. I usually write down and sketch future possibilities in a journal so that, in their multiplicity, I won't forget an important idea. Who knows, in my seventies, how many creations I may yet produce? Instead of wondering or even despairing about a brevity of time remaining, I am motivated all the more to seize the day each day, and do what I can.

## Constructing

When the design is complete, I flesh it out. I sit and stitch sometimes by machine, most usually by hand, in a contemplative frame of mind. Sometimes I fuse fabrics together with a hot iron. At this stage, resistance occasionally shows up in the hard work required and in my lack of ability. Making art quilts does not require a lot of straight machine stitching. I have a hard time with machine stitching in a straight line, as well as cutting fabric in a straight line. If I stitch two panels of a hanging, invariably one will be longer than the other because of uneven stitching. The hems won't match, the corners won't meet. I can't seem to cut pieces that match perfectly either, with scissors or with a rotary wheel cutter.

A recent experience of ineptitude came when, as a member of the Arts Team of my church, I accepted the task of making some hangings. This required extensive and precise straight cutting and stitching of ten yards of fabric. I was almost paralyzed for a month before I actually cut into the fabric. Can I really do this? I asked myself over and over, and began to search for someone else more skilled to cut and stitch than I.

My friend, Roberta Martin, also a writer, quilter and minister, rescued me. Her confidence overshadowed mine. "This is how you do it, "she said. " You fold and you cut. You fold and you cut." I watched her fold and cut with astonishment, and practiced doing it. Then gripping the fabric and scissors I forged ahead and did what was needed. The project stretched me and upon completion gave me great satisfaction. I felt confident that, if asked again, I could face straight cutting and stitching without so many qualms.

This is why art quilts have held such promise for me since I can disregard tedious precision in most of my work.

The hard work of construction can pose another challenge. When I decided to hand stitch one quilt in six strands of embroidery floss, it rebelled. The needle with its bulky thread would not go through the many layers of fabric in the quilt. I had to use needle-nose pliers to pull the needle through, resulting in a number of broken needles and blistered fingers. The quilting seemed endless. I worked on the quilt piecemeal because of my reluctance to do the labor- intensive work. Whenever I gazed at it, I sighed and murmured, "Maybe tomorrow." It hung on my design wall in various stages of completion for three years. It consumed far too much time, which provoked me to start and finish new quilts. That was beyond my customary pattern. Perhaps the energy spent in considering new pieces siphoned off required energy to finish this one. But never mind. The deadline of a quilt show I wanted to enter forced me finally to complete it.

## Showing

The last stage requires letting others see my work. This carries with it other anxieties and resistances altogether. If I enter a piece into a juried show I wonder over and over if it will be accepted. What will the judges think? I view them shaking their collective heads and moaning over what a kindergarten piece of work sits before them. Then if judges allow me to enter my work, I fall into the same rut wondering what the viewers will think. Showing our work as artists is so frightening that many avoid public viewing altogether, because we feel we are on view as well, completely naked. After my bold foray in showing *Transformation: An African Journey* for which I had positive feedback, I have discarded my resistances to exhibitions — most of the time. It depends upon the exhibition and the judges, as some impose more demands than others. If the exhibition centers around paintings and other so-called high art forms, I often hesitate to enter. But if I summon boldness, enter anyway, and my work is surprisingly accepted, I just tolerate viewers' puzzlement over my place in the show on opening night. In any case, I try to hang loose knowing that some will like my work and some will not, so I bring it out of seclusion for viewers to see, where and when I can.

Too often I meet fledgling artists who strongly resist even the possibility to engage in art let alone show it to others. If they do attempt a project they may lack courage just to let the student painter or potter sitting next to them in a class see their work. They guard it for their eyes only. They feel it's not worthy of anyone else's viewing. With a smitten demeanor, they even question, is it art? I usually respond by calling it something else: a visual expression, a heartfelt expression of their feelings and their intentions to create. An expression that is indeed worthy of acceptance "because *you* created it!" Shy artists, reluctant artists, wannabe artists need a lot of reassurance that, yes, we have something significant to contribute to humankind. We all need to understand that whatever we create even in its primordial stage has the power to influence another struggling human being. Our scraps of work, our immature artistic seedlings have the power to lift a depressed spirit, to point to a direction, and to offer insight.

Because I have been in the same swamp of self-doubt myself and know too well the burning questions about my art and its acceptance, I seek out other artists who also need reassurance. I have experienced how an affirmation from a respected source will re-ignite my smoldering creative fire. For this reason I listen to other artists' dilemmas. We share our anxieties and resistances. We determine how to manage them, because they will always be attached to our desires to make art. I explore new ways to assist the seeds of others' dreams to germinate and grow.

## Busyness

I meet resistance because of my wider involvements which tend to shut down any artistic inclinations. This happens when I get distracted, overworked or forgetful. Having a full plate day after day banishes any new thought, dream or inspiration. I cannot hear the beckoning call to create when concerns and responsibilities dominate. The inner creative fire cannot sustain me when I am invariably, insistently, inherently busy. We North Americans thrive on busyness. We wear it as a badge of honor. We are considered lazy, inept or infirm if we do not juggle six balls of commitments in the air all at once. I plead guilty along with most everyone else in our culture.

Of course with women there is always women's work, single or married. "Man's work is from sun to sun; women's work is never done," I heard while growing up. Women's work swallows us up. Everywhere our eyes fall we find 'gotta do's:' something that needs tending, wiping, cleaning, picking up or putting away. Everywhere. All the time. We shop, cook endless meals, and clean until we fall depleted into bed. Some of us are blessed with spouses who help. Even so, the burden of running a domestic domain falls heavily on our shoulders. How can I manage and be an artist, a writer, a minister? Cut back, I decide. Pile domestic chores to tackle on one day or half day a week. Let things go. As poet Carolyn Fourché is reported to have said, "Do you want a clean house or to write poetry?"

Mihaly Csikszentmihali concurs. In his book *Creativity*, he says that to remain creative we have to construct our environment to support it. Protect time, rearrange surroundings, avoid meaningless chores which leech energy out of us in order to save the energy to focus on our passion to create.

A few years ago I visited the home of Georgia O'Keeffe in Abiqui, New Mexico. It shone with stark simplicity. *There's nothing here that would distract her from painting*, I thought. *No deviations to get involved in other activities.* It probably meant that she had domestic help to cook and clean. Indeed, she had arranged her environment to support what she cared most about.

Before retirement, I served on several committees of the wider church. I visited homebound members of a congregation on a regular basis. I led spiritual formation retreats and workshops, locally and nationally. In addition, I helped in the guest house where we lived along with caring for my family. I tried to write and also to make art. Most of the outside activities warmed my heart. I had sought them eagerly and even initiated some of them. Still, they left me breathless. My adult children claimed they never could connect with either my husband or me and as a consequence gave us an answering machine one Christmas. Their assessment acted as a mirror. They have called me "the Energizer Bunny," always in motion. I could see what I was doing to my family and to myself.

I often asked myself why I crowded my schedule with what I called my "wall-to-wall days."  My days overflowed along with stuffed purses, brief cases and desk drawers that I was dreaming about at night. Was I trying to validate my ministry, my *call*, in the eyes of church authorities? Was I seeking compensatory engagement in vital things to do since my husband detached himself from me through his work? Did I simply warm to the affirmation and the socialization among like-minded associates? But look, I was becoming a workaholic, too! I scarcely admitted this, even to myself.

The result of such busyness drained me, blurred my focus, causing me to lament, *Why can't I do what I really want to do?* I was resisting settling down to write or to make art. "I'm too busy, too tired, I'm too distracted with other things" sabotaged my deepest desires. Yet, no one else imposed this on me but myself. I have met the enemy and it is me.

In retirement, I continued to take on engagements and commitments. Then I took them off, one by one. My husband, though, pointed out, "Every time you cancel an engagement or resign from a committee you take on something else in its place!" I've had to take a hard look at his assessment. When I returned from Taos, New Mexico a few years ago after an exhilarating workshop that moved me into a new direction of fabric art, I resigned from being chair of a committee. I remained on the committee but found myself doing as much work as I had done as chair. If I wanted to devote full time to my art, committee membership also had to go. I had to curb that lurking overwork, over-helping syndrome.

I have to do battle with resistances and make room for inner directives. I have to remind myself that retirement means choosing what I want to do. With the termination of work and responsibilities, an agenda-less life acts as a vacuum and sucks in other forms of busyness. An empty calendar tends to fill up quickly. I have to continually sift, discern and prioritize. Learn to say, "No." Listen to and claim the importance of dreams and artistic aspirations. They are not just a pastime, a hobby, something frivolous to be quickly displaced by more seemingly urgent commitments. *They are my life.*

I confront the words of Rilke in his *Letters to a Young Poet* when he says "Ask yourself if you must write, and if you say, 'I must,' then build your life according to this necessity." This is my challenge. Building my life congruent with my desires and my call becomes an on-going endeavor.


## Writing

When art entered my life in the early 1990s, and writing had begun to feel oppressive and life-draining, I finally abandoned it without a grain of regret. Then, in my retirement, writing again knocked on my door and asked permission to come in. I ignored it for awhile. I couldn't believe its insistence and could not believe further that I was drawn to its invitation to write about my journey into art.

Transfixed about this surprising overturn, I felt ponderous questions bearing down on me. How could I reengage in a long-term writing project with my former resistance to it still lurking over my shoulder? How could I lay aside my passionate involvement in art to spend countless hours on writing a book that might never see print? I viewed writing a book as a journey down a long road with no end in sight. Did launching a book constitute another improvisational venture into the unknown? Could I commit years to this?

These questions threatened to choke the writing aspirations that begged to emerge. The questions stood like burly guards at the door of my creativity ready to demolish me if I messed with words. I explained all this to a friend as we walked around the lake in my home town. She urged me to write the book with "Just write one little measly paragraph a day. Can't you do just that?" To write against resistance Anne Lamott suggests writing one horrendous piece that would fit into a one-inch frame. I also noted her writing practice in which she sits at her computer for fifteen minutes at a time before she's up doing something else in the house. Up and down, throughout the day, but mastering resistance against never finishing. She gets the job done, piece by piece, overcoming hesitations, stalling and restlessness. But neither Lamott's nor my friend's advice jump-started me. I felt no compulsion to sit at my computer and pound out words. I had no inner necessity. I concluded that only God could generate the motivation I needed.

I shared my dilemma about writing with Roberta. She lit a candle to honor our gathering. "This is holy time," she said. She saw my need for encouragement to write. She did not view writing and art as an either/or proposition in my life. "They are coming together. Something new is being born," she affirmed. "Yes," I said. "They have come full circle."

The sacred moment inspired me deeply. I hired a writing coach, Peggy Millen, who further motivated me. Her feedback and encouragement helped me to overcome my resistances. I slowly, intently pulled words out of myself onto paper. Gradually the verbal dam broke and words began to flow. In a spiritual direction session, Sister Loretta declared, "If you are writing again, it must be from God!"

Initially, I wasn't sure about how to frame the writing. A work book? A fictionalized account? My personal story? In sharing my quandary about directions, Cathy Kapikian of Wesley Seminary urgently pleaded with me to write a personal narrative. "You must tell your story," she said. "Art has given you so much joy. You must share this!"

Still, sparks of resistance refused to be extinguished. I wrestled with their cause. My reservations seemed to boil down to no guarantee of end results. A launching into deep waters and letting my net down with just misty hopes for my effort. In Luke's Gospel, Peter was commanded by Jesus to do just this after a night of fruitless fishing. He must have thought his carpenter friend naïve at best. But Peter followed Jesus' crazy command, probably with eyes rolled upward and a shaking of the head. Overwhelming results followed, with an excessive number of fish breaking their nets.

Instead of great end results, fickleness may intrude. Couples marry with great expectations and a hoped-for happy life together. That may or may not happen. Students overcome mountains of study and writing in graduate school and then may not find employment in their field. Expected opportunities seem to vanish. It takes determination to do the hard work, no matter the results, along with a great leap of faith to aim for successful outcomes.

I began to realize that outcome throttled any desire to write. I again engaged in an imaginary conversation with a friend:

Me: "Why spend hours and hours, weeks and months at a project that may never get beyond my computer?"

Friend: "You mean you don't like to do something without knowing what will come of it?"

Me: "Exactly. I don't have years and years of life ahead of me. I need to use the time wisely. I mean, you know the odds of getting published. No one may ever read what I've written after all this time spent working on the book. Suppose

I'm the only one to read my work! What a waste of time."

Friend: "Why should it be a waste if nothing comes of it except for your own personal benefit?"

Me: "What do you mean?"

Friend: "Suppose your writing brings forth long hidden remembrances and flashes of insight previously lost to you but which you need to recapture? Suppose you need to write this book for reasons you may never understand or for persons you may never know, but God's wisdom understands and that is why God has called you to do it? Do you always have to figure out God's intentions?"

Me: "Well, I try!"

Friend: "Just let go, Martha Jane. View your writing as a spiritual practice. Remember what Thomas Merton said: he could 'disappear' into his writing, make it a prayer, and he wouldn't let results concern him."

Me: "But he had plenty of publication results — wide spread results. And he had no intention to publish?"

Friend: "No, but I think his superiors in the monastery insisted that he write. They saw his gift. He saw writing not so much as responding to them but to God, and being faithful to God."

Me: "I recall also how he initially responded to God by entering Gethsemani Monastery in Kentucky. I remember the awesome words engraved on that gate when he walked through it to enter: 'God Alone.' They often stop me."

Friend: "Hmm. Perhaps with that mindset he was able to incorporate that intentionality and focus into his writing."

Me: "With that mindset, if he were responding to God alone as the audience, the reader, the ruminator over his writing, then nothing else would matter."

Friend: "Exactly!"

It seemed that responding faithfully to a Call counted more than what product or result emerged. I laid the facts on the table: I felt a sense of Call to write the book whatever it entailed. I would respond to that Call as faithfully as I could, day after day at my computer, and throw outcomes to the wind. I would be writing the book as a response to God and to follow God's directive.

An old non-scriptural story tells of Jesus who asked his disciples to carry some large stones to a river. Peter picked up the biggest he could find, thinking he was contributing to some great project. With great effort he walked with the others to the river, struggling and breathing heavily all the way. At river's edge, Jesus commanded the twelve to drop their stones into the water. They did. They brushed off their hands, and in a few moments turned their puzzled faces towards their Master, with the word "Why?" written all over them. When Jesus had their undivided attention he asked, "For whom were you carrying the stones?"

I have envisioned the words, *God Alone*, engraved on my computer desk. It answers my repeated fervent question, "For whom are you writing this book?"

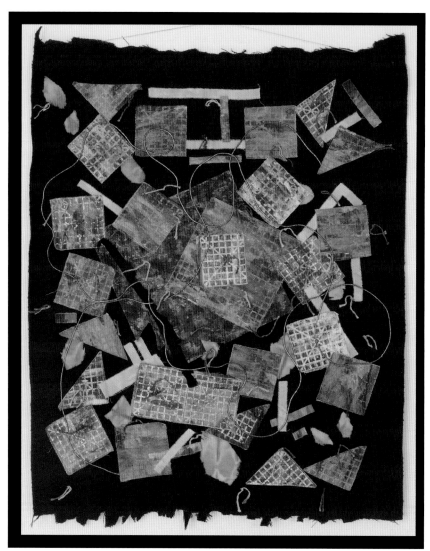

**DANCE IN THE DARKNESS**
32" x 23"

*"My quilt was resisting me
and I was resisting it."*

# 10

# COURAGE FOR ARTISTIC CHALLENGES

As North Americans our identity is tethered to what we produce. I didn't realize this until I lived outside our borders for sixteen years. Africa taught me its go-slow mode which reduced my usual stir-crazy productivity. There, I chucked my calendar because I could easily remember the few engagements needing attention. But living in the United States, a crowded agenda pervades my life. My self-identity comes under scrutiny if I am not forever on-the-go and can show nothing I have produced, designed or created. Who am I apart from what I do? That question particularly goads me and others when we have left our usual workplace, whether laid-off or retired. A woman recently retired from an active counseling ministry lamented to me, "I have nothing to do. I don't know who I am anymore!" Although I clearly and thankfully have something to do, as an artist I fall prey to the identity question as I face my blank design wall: *Who am I to be creating art out of fabric? What makes me think I am an artist?* I ask. These questions and my initial lack of a design, a process or a beginning point stymie my intentions to produce a quilt even though passion fires me to do so.

As I stand at my work table considering what to do, the quiet of my studio and my stilled actions and thoughts fly in the face of the buzzing, stirring life beyond me. Art making requires such stillness in order to summon the creative muse. Creating art, though, seems so countercultural, even non-essential. "Get busy, get busy, don't just stand there: do something!" the culture drums in my ears. At times I am tempted to burst outside and immerse myself in an action recognized as worthwhile. Wouldn't that be of more value? I recognize the temptation posed to me to belittle my work as an artist. Firmly setting my resolve, I tune out these intruding whispers and turn to my creative work.

Writing discharges its own anxious questions. When I sit down to write, the blank computer screen unnerves me. Words lie waiting to spring to the page, but I cannot seem to pull them up. What do I want to say? Where do I begin? Are my words worth anything at all? Is the time consumed in a writing project worth the expenditure?  Am I a writer or not? Self-doubt haunts me and frequently paralyzes me.

Occasionally — perhaps only occasionally — the void, the empty page or canvas, the untouched clay captivates us. These unformed artistic possibilities may beg us to engage them, to relate to them, to create something with them. The need to make order out of chaos may rise up within us. On the other hand, such emptiness may create a paralyzing fear. Vincent Van Gogh spoke of the terror of a blank canvas, "It sits there and says to the artist: You don't know anything!" What does it take to get past fear and to begin painting or shaping or stitching? Might we reach a point where bravery and creative urges will overcome resistances to begin?

Sometimes delving into another medium will help launch the innate creativity deep inside. Instead of composing a poem, one might try composing music. The fabric artist can cross over to pottery, the potter to watercolor, the landscape architect to photography. Engaging in unfamiliar methods, palettes and patterns will awaken the child within, one without inhibitions who loves to play. And play can open doors to unexpected and exciting new work.

When I feel empty of ideas, two pieces of advice have spurred me to proceed with my fabric art process. One is: make visual decisions visually. I do this when I "audition" fabrics in my studio for possible inclusion. I rarely make sketches of what to do and where to go with a piece. I certainly don't dream up compositions lying in bed at night or walking around my town's lake.

Flashes of insight may come then, but I cannot figure out a design only by thinking about it. I have to see possibilities. I see what goes together in terms of colors and fabric designs. I scatter fabric pieces around my studio on tables, chairs, stools and on my design wall to see what works best. Up close I scrutinize several pieces. Then I stand back to view the results as a whole, a back and forth movement as I proceed. I evaluate my choices visually and thereby move forward.

The second piece of advice is: start small. When it comes to writing, Anne Lamott suggests writing only one tiny paragraph at a time because, "we're not trying to scale up a glacier," all at once. Fabric artists frequently start small with snips of fabrics glued to a card or into a sketchbook. Sometimes I doodle with them at my work table while talking on the phone. Additionally, I start small when I take half or whole yards of fabric, fold them, and pin them to my design wall. I examine the effect. By folding and pinning, I forgo cutting any fabrics until I have made final choices. This step reduces waste and prevents deep regrets from mistakes and misjudgments. If I do cut yardage then decide not to use it in a specific design, with restrained weeping and gnashing of teeth I store the cut pieces in a plastic bag for later use. After all, quilts and collages are generally created from scraps.

I have discovered a third way to overcome a creative void, a bold, uninhibited way. I collect some fabric scraps or colored photos cut from magazines, or I sweep papers with paint. I move them around on my table or design wall, usually in tune with vigorous CD music. I don't plan or think of what I am doing. I take improvisation to its height in this exercise, following my intuition as to what to include and which way to go. Courageously engaging the unknowns of play, I have not worried about results. I usually end up with a flamboyant yet exciting muddle but one which has subdued my hesitations and apprehensions to begin a new quilt.

At rock bottom, I must summon courage to encounter the blank page, the unformed lump of clay, the pieces of vibrant cloth waiting to be formed into an art piece, seemingly from nothing.

Because art making involves unmitigated misunderstanding, it remains marginal in our society, frequently eliminated when schools and communities cut their budgets. Artists are viewed as different, out of touch with reality, and puzzling objects, if not crazy or weird. We may hear, or imagine we hear from others, "You are a phony, you have no talent, you'll waste paper, ink, clay, paint, fabric in your middling efforts to make art. Who are you to remove yourself from the world's ills, hide out in a studio and put your work on display?"

On top of such outer assessments, artists' inner negative voices are no less damaging. *I'm not good enough. I don't have what it takes in terms of perseverance or skill. I'm not a real artist — just making a feeble effort to act like one. I don't have the proper credentials. Am I making a fool of myself?*

I have heard all those assessments and voices. Still, I persisted on a road to art making. Perhaps my age gave me courage. I could care less about what people thought about my unusual journey into art at age 65. More than this, however, I began to explore earlier years in my life when I had to rely on courage. Seeing its presence weaving in and out of challenging circumstances empowered me to navigate through each one, and then into art making late in life.

In an art workshop I recently constructed a small journal using photos of trees. In a few pages I reviewed facets of my life supported by courage. Under the photo of a lone tree towering over other treetops, I wrote: "There in that gawky age harbored strength and resilience which transformed me with 'courage' and 'adventure' as my middle names ... standing out against their expectations: stark, tall and alone."  Although I grew up as a treasured kid in a warm southern home, I nevertheless forged my own path. I resisted presumptions that I enter the social scene by coming out as a debutante. I chose nursing as a career when my father and some college faculty members viewed it as demeaning. Under more tree photographs I wrote, "Courage to stand alone... Courage to bend with the wind... Courage to nest little ones in my branches... Courage to paint, to quilt, to write..."

Other events came to mind:

- From grades One through Seven, I moved eleven different times in elementary school, due to my father's frequent relocation in his work. In new classrooms, I had to overcome strangeness, a sense of not belonging, a lot of stares at this newcomer trying to show a brave face.

- My parents did not accompany me and my stuff when I entered my freshman year in college so I could prove to myself that I could go it alone.

- At midnight in June between my junior and senior years in college I flew alone out of the Charlotte, NC airport to Mexico to volunteer in a mission hospital for the summer, knowing no one there who would receive me.

- Alone again, at age twenty-one I traveled to New York city by train to attend nursing school for three years in an imposing hospital of that city. My friends' non-understanding over my choice to pursue nursing after a vigorous four academic years accentuated my sense of aloneness.

- At age twenty-four, I flew to Scotland to marry my true love who was studying there and whom I had not seen for a year.

- Courage accompanied me again when I settled with my husband and three small children — all born overseas — into the unknowns of mission work in Ghana for ten years.

- During our years in Taiwan and in West Africa, I — both daring and naïve — found myself doing things I never thought in a hundred years I'd do because no one else could or would do them. At eight months pregnant I conducted a Taiwanese student choir, knowing only the music but not the language in which they sang. In Ghana, because of school needs I preached in Ghanaian high school compulsory Sunday vespers regularly.

- Since nursing opportunities vanished for me in Africa, preaching and teaching opportunities arose. This led to my setting foot on a seminary campus back home to begin Greek and the arduous road to ordination as a Presbyterian minister at age 48. I again reached for courage and gratefully found it.

With astonishment as I reviewed my life history I realized that courage resided in my very cells as an intimate component. I frequently gripped it with white- knuckled hands, motivated only by trust in God and by Jesus' willingness to endure the unspeakable. Courage strengthened my desire to help those in need, aided by promising adventure, irresistible opportunities, intriguing neighborhoods and foreign cultures.

Courage to make art increased as I studied other women artists who endured personal pain and misunderstanding far more than I. Still, their lives and persistence inspire me. Present-day artist Judy Chicago faced humiliation and scathing misunderstanding over and over from her feminist art. She felt that the arts community was "Dead set against me," primarily because she was female and depicted female issues, notably *The Dinner Party* which made her both famous and infamous. She still persisted although tempted at several points to lay down her paint brush. "But I will never be persuaded that it is time to put aside my art, for it has made my life worth living," she said.

Georgia O'Keeffe's work of the last century also faced vast misunderstanding as viewers read female sexual symbols into her large paintings of flowers. She said, "It takes courage to be a painter. I have walked on the edge of a knife." Although she studied at the Art Institute of Chicago and the Art Students League in New York, she lamented the emphasis in copying the style of Old Masters. Finally in 1915 she boldly struck out on her own. She said, "I have things in my head that are not like what anyone has taught me — shapes and ideas so near to me — so natural to my way of thinking.... I decided to start anew — to strip away what I had been taught — to accept as true my own thinking."

Kathe Kollwitz (1857-1945) of Germany courageously protested the inhumanity of poverty, injustice and war through her lithographs, drawings and sculpture. Through her work she felt "A responsibility of being an advocate ... and to voice the sufferings." Her raw depictions of poor mothers with hungry children personify the devastating disease and famine in Germany at the time of the First and Second World Wars and the rise of the National Socialist Party inflamed by Hitler. That regime declared her work as "degenerate." She eventually was forced to resign from her professorship at the Prussian Academy of Arts. By 1936 her work was banned and never seen in public again. Her intense grief at the death of her son in the first war and a grandson in the second spilled out in more drawings and lithographs to reflect not only her own suffering but that of all women around her. A bomb destroyed remnants of her work along with her house in Berlin in 1943, followed by similar destruction of the home of her son Hans and his wife a week later. She wrote to them, "Oh, God, life is hard. Keep up your courage."

Frieda Kahlo (1907-1954) suffered physically all her life from an accident riding a bus in her teens. She underwent 35 surgeries to mend more than 15 broken, crushed and dislocated bones. Restricted in mobility all her life and lying in bed or in a wheel chair she painted herself in 55 portraits since, she said, "I am often alone and I am the object I know best." Her pain both from her physical trauma plus the emotional devastation over her husband's philandering seemed to fuel her painting. She rendered several rather grotesque images of her broken heart and body. Her *The Broken Column* depicts her tears along with one of several fierce corsets she had to wear for her broken back. Her *Tree of Hope, Keep Firm* was painted after one of seven surgeries for her back. On the left side of the painting the viewer sees her prone, weakened body with gaping red surgical incisions on her back, and on the right, the seated, well dressed, strong Frieda, with a spinal corset in her hand and holding a flag with the words of the title as if to rev up courage and hope. Her husband, famed muralist Diego Rivera, lauded her courage and said of her: "Frieda is the only example in the history of art of an artist who tore open her chest and her heart to reveal the biological truth of her feelings."

Courage enabled these women to tolerate rejection of their art, to insistently resist the norms of the art world and in the culture around them, and to bring to life their artistic passions no matter the obstacles. The challenges in my life pale in comparison to these artists of courage. Nevertheless, I absorbed important lessons and ideas from their artistic careers:

— From Judy Chicago, I have indeed resonated with how life-giving art was to her, and how it has been to me, with no desire to bring it to a halt.

— From Georgia O'Keeffe, I too have struck out on my own, leaving behind traditional ideas on how to create my art, as she did.

— Frieda Kahlo painted her feelings within the restrictions of bodily and emotional trauma, which I never experienced. Yet, my feelings are revealed in the colors of my quilts and have fueled my passion to create more of them.

— Kathe Kollwitz became an advocate for the suffering around her through her art. I, too, want to focus my future work toward a social issue, notably the loss of the beautiful environment around us through human ignorance and willful neglect.

While trying to find my path in art making, a friend said to me, "It takes a great deal of courage to follow your own track and to move away from conventional ones." Indeed, courage enabled me to depart from non-parish ministry to nurture others in their faith as a spiritual guide beyond any local congregation. It supported me to create my own distinctive collage art with fabric. In spite of my burning questions to the contrary, I did so without credentials or approval from friendly advisors or powers-that-be. I heard ringing in my ears the phrase from *The Little Engine That Could:* "I think I can, I think I can, I think I can." I simply pushed ahead with my inner fire and an innate sense of color and design.

Hearing how local artists around me have overcome their fears and resistances to make art have deeply inspired me to create my own work. I don't have to go it alone — I can receive new energy from those who have overcome obstacles, along with criticisms and who have grown to trust their ability to make art. Being a part of group art making not only builds up one's own confidence to make art but affords opportunities to learn new and valuable techniques and perspectives.

Additionally, non-artist friends have encouraged me when I hear how they have confronted and overcome obstacles. Like getting back on a horse after a fall from the saddle a week earlier. Like being afraid of heights, yet climbing up a canyon path, refraining from looking down at the abyss all the way up. Or confronting a negligent but powerful head of a school board. Or leaving security and a steady income in order to leave a dead marriage. Or walking on your own all around the supermarket after painful spinal surgery. When I hear of these examples I am enabled to move out from my own hesitations and apprehensions. It takes minimal exploration to uncover courage on many fronts right in my neighborhood.

The deepest fear in making art is that of self-revelation. My writing or my visual expressions will invariably reveal my thoughts and feelings. Through my art renditions others can partially peer into my soul. I wonder, *Am I brave enough to offer such exposure? Am I vulnerable enough?* As Robert Piepenburg has said "Our love of ourselves and all that we hold dear is what gives us the courage to act without fear of consequence. It is what allows us the freedom to sing, dance, act, paint or whatever, *as if nobody is watching* (italics mine)." If I shrink at putting my thoughts and feelings on display, my freedom to make art will disappear. I will then create only safe compositions readily accepted by others. Yet with the cultivation of courage and self-assurance I can indeed create my best with abandon  and not worry who "is watching."

It seems to me that trust underlies the cultivation of courage. Not trust that every stitch, stroke or word will smoothly emerge. Not trust that I will never waste precious resources and must start over. Not trust that I will always finish what I start. Rather a God-inspired trust and self-confidence that deep within me stirs the flame of creativity which will flare up in its own good time. A trust that with God's help and direction I can keep on keeping on, no matter what messes I make in my art or in life's complexities. In every venture, God gives me the wherewithal to support me in whatever I need, not necessarily in the way of provisions or ideas, but certainly in God's *presence* to calm my fears and to stiffen my resolve.

## Stretching Beyond Our Scope

When artists are given a commission to produce a project others desire, a whole different kind of courage is required. Suppose we are asked to produce a *magnum opus* which will stretch our imaginations and skills to the limit? A call to follow an untried, even scary path but one which we feel impelled to walk?

My ultimate stretching came when Montreat's Conference Center in North Carolina invited me to create a large quilt for their Inn. Being paid for this effort ramped up my sense of responsibility. A price was put on the end result before it even appeared. Those paying me held great assumptions that I could produce what they wanted. Could I indeed do so? Further, if I am paid to do the work, I cannot make a mess, either in figuring the costs of my supplies or in the finished product. The public and prominent display of the quilt bore heavily down on me. Others would see it, others would judge it, and others would accept or reject it. Being thrilled and honored interlaced with anxiety and made me pause over this my first commission. I knew I was the one to create the artwork since staff in Montreat had affirmed my fabric art in different conference settings. But to create something so huge, so permanent and so intricate unnerved me. Could I rise to the occasion?

The finished piece would hang from the ceiling over the empty space of a stairway which meant both front and back would be viewed. The space required a work larger than I had ever created, but how large? Because it would dangle in mid-air, I could not take measurements against a wall. I simply guessed that it needed to be five feet by seven feet by measuring a railing underneath where it would hang. The uncertainty of my calculations unnerved me. Would it be large enough for the space and how would the piece hang in it? I shuddered as I tried to imagine how the end result would look.

I was given no guidelines to make the quilt except it must blend in with the Inn's color scheme of burgundy, forest green, tan and gold with sparks of bright aqua. On my own I decided on a theme of nature within the mountain setting in which Montreat sits. I also determined to make the quilt in three panels with the center one a bit longer than the two side ones. This would not only make the piece easier to handle in construction but would add more interest to the composition.

I slowly conceived a direction on how to progress in making the quilt, totally different from my usual improvisational art making. I had to envision a design, have it approved by those who had commissioned me and demonstrate where I was going with it. I could not meander along the way, being guided by intuition when I create my own work. Never before had others' expectations influenced my work. It took courage to accept such a project formulated by other people and to have an end result in mind before I ever cut into the fabric.

Aside from measurements and colors, I initially created a folder with samples of fabric and cut-outs of interesting designs and techniques featured in quilting magazines. I began to look at fabric possibilities from vendors at the usual August Asheville Quilt Show and collected a few samples. I saw several for inclusion from quilt shops in Wytheville, Virginia and Marietta, Georgia along with North Carolina quilt shops in Asheville and Black Mountain. I finally decided on a fabric for the background of the center panel: an abstract design of green and burgundy trees sold in the Wytheville shop. Stopping there in October, I bought several yards of it along with other fabrics for the side panels. As the clerk kept unrolling bolt after bolt, I trembled. I had never bought so much yardage at once.

With unsteady hands I bravely made the first cut into the fabric for the center panel. *Did I really know what I was beginning?* Anxieties, fears and nervousness swept over me. My palms sweated. *Could I pull this off?* I made that initial cut in Montreat's craft shop on its large tables. No space in my home — not even in my studio — would accommodate the dimensions of the quilt. As usual I had difficulty cutting in a straight line. Later I wondered why I had not torn the fabric since that always assures a straight edge. Did the space constraints at home mean that I had to go back and forth to the craft shop, three miles away, to create this quilt?

My imaginative and very supportive husband came up with a brilliant solution: turn our living room into a temporary studio. We removed the coffee table and replaced that space with fifty-five gallon drums brought up from the basement (used years previously to ship household goods to Africa and back). Over the drums he placed large pieces of plywood. It made a table surface just the right height for cutting and fusing the pieces together. Also from the basement Pete brought up leftover pieces of insulation panels we painted for my design wall which we leaned against the doors into the den. Fabric could be easily attached to the soft panels. I put a sturdy piece of cardboard across the sofa, setting it on the arms at either end. On it I arranged my fabrics by color groups. The upholstered chairs also accommodated differing fabrics of sheers and metallics. With the addition of my Featherweight sewing machine placed on the dining table, my ironing board and iron within reach, plus CD's to soothe or energize me, my new studio was complete. Every time I entered it during the course of the project, I sat down, gazed at the colors on all sides, reveled in the music I played, and smiled. I experienced deep contentment and nourishment by the scene before me. Truly art making had become my spiritual practice. It centered me and led me to joy which, in turn, emboldened my progress.

The biggest challenge meant narrowing down options among the multitude of images which surfaced and begged to be included in the quilt. Everywhere I looked I saw delightful possibilities: in nature, in paintings, in others' quilts, or in photographs. (Even the rough green-gray walls of mountain peaks in a Yosemite photograph grabbed me. With artist's eyes, everything is absorbed. At every turn and at most times a visual assault pierce's the artist's vision and creativity.)  I wanted to express myself in so many colors and techniques, objects and designs. The profusion of ideas initially stumped me. But of course I had to make choices to include this option and to exclude that one. How to decide? I considered attending the huge quilt fest in Houston held every November. But my friend Roberta said, "You don't need to do that. This quilt is already inside you." Slowly I agreed. At the fest, I would see even more options and possibilities which would leave me more dazzled and confused. Finally,

I determined a rudimentary design, presented it to the Montreat staff for approval in November and was on my way. In January, construction began.

Originally, the Conference Center wanted me to include its slogan in the quilt: *Strengthening Churches, Building Relationships, Growing Disciples.* I had not anticipated this wrinkle. I even asked "Is this quilt a marketing tool?" "Well, of course," came the reply which left me somewhat disgruntled. I therefore spent some time to learn how to letter on fabric by talking with Robyn Josephs who had experience and tools for lettering, plus buying a book to glean more ideas. Much to my relief, the slogan evaporated. The new President of the Center told me in January to scrap the idea: that my creation would be considered as an art piece alone.

After I pinned the fabric for the centerpiece to my new design wall, my first action was to cut out a small mountain range in aqua, turquoise and gold for the top. The mountains would eventually extend across the two side panels, creating continuity. I cut them out and fused them down with my iron. I had to stand on a stool to pin them to the top of the panel. I then wove on the center panel torn strips of burgundy, shades of green, khaki and gold, plus pieces of leftover upholstery from the Inn's lobby furniture. I stamped some of the strips or embellished them with beads or stitching. In the spaces between the strips I inserted natural objects such as sticks, mica, images of ferns, trees and flowers stamped on fabric, plus symbols representing Montreat. I included actual rhododendron leaves, rolled up like cigars from a winter's cold, sprayed them with a fixative and placed them near the top out of reach from curious fingers.

I needed a central image as a focus for the center panel. I pondered what to include. At first I tried a large spiral of golden toned tan. But after perusing quilting magazines and books the image of a bird's nest caught my eye. I cut out tan and gold fabrics in long curved strips for the straw in the nest. I fused it all down in a semi-circular pattern, placing a dark maroon piece in its center to highlight the emptiness of the nest. I deliberately wanted viewers to imagine for themselves its contents. I placed the nest on a brown tree branch with a profusion of multi-shaded green leaves descending downward. At the end of one cascade of leaves I placed a small cross of an unusual shape. The quilt needed a Christian symbol, I figured, but not one of enormous dimensions to immediately attract attention. It had to be there but subtly placed.

The two side panels — which would hang separately from the center one — stayed in flux frustratingly long. I experimented with a diagonal composition of various fabrics over the lighter toned side panels, but discarded the idea. I tried vertical strips on the panels interspersed with what I called *cameos*, squares of stylistic natural objects configured in fabric. This arrangement did not work either. Finally in a heavy book of art quilts my friend Connie had sent me I hit upon the right idea, adapting an image in the book by turning it on its side. I stamped, stitched and appliquéd images in small rectangles of fabric, setting them at angles in the side panels. The rectangles were centered around a large light green piece of fabric stamped with a live fern in one instance and a curly vine in another.

Finally the day arrived to put everything together. Instead of inserting batting (a cushiony inner lining) between the front and the back I chose to eliminate this step by backing the quilt with a piece of heavy upholstery. It took a degree of courage to choose this path as I had never before heard of doing this. I even sought reassurance from some sister quilters on this technique and with that, moved forward. After attaching the front to the back with pins, I tried stitching the panels on my sewing machine but it would not accept the heavy layers. I attempted to sew the front to the back by hand. The fabrics bunched up at every interval. A smooth surface resisted me. I had reached an impasse and was devastated. How could I go forward? *Take heart, take heart,* I mused. *There must be a way.*

A noted Asheville quilter from whom I had taken a class came to mind, Norma Bradley. I emailed her about my dilemma and she responded that day saying I should call her. I did and explained the predicament more fully. She invited me to her studio the next day. I was astonished at her quick and generous response. There she showed me how to fuse down the layers first before stitching the panels with the machine. Her immediate assistance has made me eternally grateful to her. I could not have proceeded without her help.

I stitched the side panels but the center panel — again because of the thickness — would not submit to my machine. My only option came in tying the layers of the panel together with colorful threads placed about two inches apart. On a Saturday, Robyn helped me tie the quilt with 140 pieces of embroidery floss. After that, binding the raw edges of the three panels remained, which the owner of the local quilt shop had agreed to do. But when I arrived at her shop with the panels and the fabric for binding, other concerns had overtaken her, so she taught me how to do the work then and there on her machine. Again the thickness of the center panel balked both in her and my sewing machines. I could only stitch binding for the side panels. With another quilter's recommendation, I hired Roma Wimberley to do the work on a heavier machine which she possessed. I then had to blind stitch the 590 inches of the binding on the underside by hand which seemed to take forever. I finished at 10:00 p.m. on July 28, 2009. Photographing it by Perrin Todd took place and then hanging at the Inn the next day.

Anxiety overwhelmed me waiting to see how the pieces would hang from the large pole I had bought in an Asheville store. Would the quilt fit the space? Would the three panels hang evenly? With great relief everything swung from the ceiling beautifully and harmoniously. I had invited friends for the hanging event, especially those who had helped me. Spontaneously, Roberta offered a prayer of dedication. The quilt received a lot of publicity, adulation and comments. One person said, "You pulled out all the stops." Indeed, indeed. I was overcome with gratitude for the courage which empowered my perseverance to complete the year-long, arduous process. I named the quilt *Mountain Retreat*. At home, I sank down in great relief and, with Pete, offered a celebratory prayer of ardent thanksgiving.

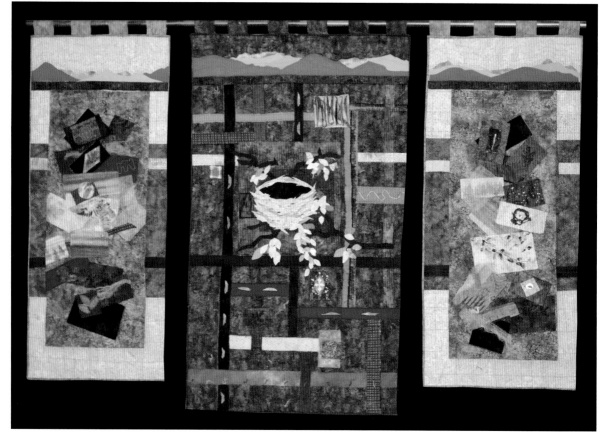

**MOUNTAIN RETREAT**
**5' X 7'**

*"The maroon empty center of the nest invites viewers to imagine its contents."*

# 11

## OVERFLOW INTO A VISUAL MINISTRY

One night, in the basement of Decatur, Georgia's Columbia Presbyterian Church, eight of us sat around a table. It was January 1997 and I was facilitating our group in going through *The Artist's Way: A Spiritual Path to Higher Creativity* by Julia Cameron. The group consisted of a struggling writer in his eighties, a landscape architect, a piano/organ player who taught music, a dabbler in pottery, a business editor, and two others trying to pump up their creative juices. Our mutual enthusiasm sustained us through twelve long weeks of Cameron's arduous exercises and questions.

I relished the program as much as anyone. I found Cameron's recommended "artist's dates" thrilling. This meant going alone on weekly excursions to feast our eyes and feed our souls. I eagerly spent my dates in galleries, flea markets, craft shops, movies and a flower show. The ventures enhanced my noticing of more and more inventive and imaginative objects. I learned what made compositions harmonious, and how artists melded contrary media together. I discovered a thousand possibilities for designs in glass, chairs, floral arrangements, shoes, stitchery and ways to frame pictures.

One exercise in *The Artist's Way* directed us to make autobiographical collages of past events and future dreams. We did this together in class with the stacks of magazines, scissors, paste and poster board I had brought. Each person worked with determination after which we circled around to hear what each creator had to say about his or her piece and then we commented on what we noticed in it.

In my collage I included the predictable parts of myself: my life in Africa, my family, my spiritual connection with God represented by a woman walking on a swinging bridge, my dreams for our future retirement home. A cutout quote — "Who is that lady?" — reflected my continuing quandary about my vocation and gifts. Among the pasted down magazine photos I included one of people viewing quilts in a gallery. The reason for this photo escaped me until I heard myself say to the group as they gathered to view my creation, "Some day I would like to exhibit my work."

My words so stunned me that I wondered if I had said them. At the time, my work consisted of two lone quilts. Where did these words and the inclusion of the photo come from, and what did they mean? A hidden, unconscious dream had shot to the surface. I didn't want just to view others' quilts or just create quilts. I wanted to show my quilts. Image making had unleashed a hidden longing from my unconscious. I deeply desired to share my art. Little did I know that within two years my dream would bear fruit and I would be exhibiting my work.

Leading *The Artist's Way* energized me. I loved watching the participants overcome barriers to their creativity. Kindling their emerging creative fires revved up my own flame to leap higher.

"I'm going to make time intentionally for my own piano enrichment," said the musician.

"I'm going to write an article a week on something I like, not something I'm just assigned," said the editor.

"I don't know where this is taking me," said another. "But I'm going to keep exploring."

And I said, "I'm going to try to facilitate more groups, and encourage creativity in individuals as part of my ministry."

"Go for it!" came the response.

I had to ask myself: *why this urgency to share my art and carry my emerging quilts out into public space?* I asked myself more questions:

> *Do I need approval of my art from others?*
>
> *Do I want to inspire others who view my quilts and influence people's perspectives??*
>
> *Do I want honest feedback which will enhance future quilts that I make?*
>
> *Do I have a message in my art which longs to be heard?*
>
> *Do I want to sell my work and make money from it?*
>
> *Do I want to dialogue with other persons about the art making experience?*

The questions prodded me. I could partly say Yes to all but the desire to sell my work. They were not to be dismissed lightly.

Since art can soothe troubled persons or revitalize sagging spirits or proclaim a prophetic message, *what do I want my art to accomplish?* This took time to consider.

## Art in Church Settings

Opportunities to share my art and art making experiences with others slowly began to pop open in Columbia Church. I had been given an upstairs room in which to paint. This gracious gift of the studio room had been dropped into my life as if God had arranged it. I wondered why. I had hoped that my presence would act as catalyst to awaken creative energies in the congregation.

By early 1998, the church invited me to be Parish Associate for Art in the Church. It was just the right place for me to do art, for through my previous experience with them as their Interim Minister, they loved me. I recalled the words of Joan of Sausalito CA whom I met at the Visual Arts conference in

1995: "You need to do art in a church where, when you fall, they will pick you up." Indeed, the members of this church would gladly pick me up. I had this reassurance when I responded in joy to their offer.

As Parish Associate for Art, I facilitated a design for the church logo, guided banner making, helped with props for dramas and taught an adult Sunday class on art in the life of the church. I led an alternative class to the usual Wednesday night Bible study, called "Encountering God through Prayer, Art and Creativity," and an art component for adults in the Vacation Bible School for a week in the summer. I also shared prints of Christ in a discussion with adults on "Who is Jesus?"

The younger adults in the congregation could not attend most of my offerings. Although they expressed keen interest, they spent time and energy in programs for their children. The older adults were not risk takers, nor had they ever engaged in putting markers to paper in a church setting. So, only three or four joined my efforts. In one class, after I explained the visual expressions we would be making, a member jumped to her feet, exclaiming, "I can't do this! I'm outta here!" Others dropped by the wayside, leaving one member in the class. I nevertheless persevered, and so did he. The Associate Minister said to me later, "Don't be discouraged with what happened in that class. Your one student was touched so very deeply."

I soon realized that not everyone shared my enthusiasm. Some resonated with art, others resisted it. Art making can be threatening to some. I wondered if there were subversive ways to capture people before their fears snared them. If ways existed among most of the congregation, I never found them. I learned that some people simply won't respond to someone else's passion, no matter how electrifying or articulate or well-planned the appeal. I learned something important.

While making art with persons in Columbia Church, I helped initiate art at my Seminary. After sharing with the President my enthusiasm for art in a theological setting, he helped establish a committee to introduce art into the Seminary. Artists, ministers, staff and faculty members participated in the committee. We began with juried exhibitions held in the Continuing Education Center. Twice we featured an arts week in the spring term, highlighting jazz on the quadrangle, poetry readings, Saturday workshops, and a communion service incorporating dance, music and visual art.

I couldn't believe that a dream had materialized in this heavy academic setting.

## Leading Art Retreats

I continued attending the art retreats at the convent in Lantana, Florida. There, my spiritual life and my artistic self became permanently sealed together. Prayer had literally intertwined with paint. I saw how Elizabeth, the leader, had facilitated this. I saw how to combine art with the spiritual life, with prayer and sharing in a retreat setting. A thought held me captive: *why not lead these kinds of retreats yourself?* Villa International would be the perfect location for such an event.

Some months later during Lent, I offered *Painting the Passion*, with great trepidation. I alone was the facilitator of a retreat, not a participant, and I felt as insecure as a kid learning to swim. Who was I to do this, I pondered. This echoed the same question when I showed my first quilt, *Transformation*, in the Sue Monk Kidd event years earlier. I had led only the one retreat on creativity at Montreat Conference Center which I described previously and had participated in a few workshops and three art retreats in Lantana. With limited qualifications I nevertheless figured that my zeal to share the power of art with others would count for something. I reassured myself that I had the ability to organize the flow of the time together and knew how to connect vital spiritual themes with art making. I advertised in the local weekly newspaper and spread news of the event among friends and acquaintances. Eight persons came. We worked in paint and collage with themes concerning Christ's passion. I took phrases from the Gospel accounts of his passion, like "he was sorrowful and troubled," "the disciples forsook him and fled," and "Why have you forsaken me?" With fervor, we imaged the quotations abstractly. I noted each participant's rash hunger to make art. The courage required to offer and to lead the retreat bloomed in joyful results.

Later I co-led an Advent retreat with Mary Logan, a pastoral counselor and gifted artist. We entitled it *Holy Darkness: Waiting and Birthing.* The flyer said; "We will take time to linger, ponder, wait and wonder in a meditation process that will include poetry and prayer, scripture and singing. Choices for visual expression include beads for praying, containers for holding, and accordion books for gazing." A dozen women participated. Pausing from the rush of Christmas preparations to absorb stillness, the group exhaled deeply to drop their exhausting burdens. They expressed their need for holy darkness and enlivening possibilities. We focused on the Magnificat, and words inspired by John of the Cross's *Dark Night.*

Then the lunge towards art making. The impatience to put hands to work: crafting, baking and stringing beads, assembling colored boxes, pasting and folding collaged papers. The fever to do it all. The thirst to make something, to give form to things not seen. The women didn't want to leave. They begged for more retreats.

We led another retreat called *Passing Over: Making Art to Express Brokenness and Hope in a Lenten Retreat.* During this one, participants created three-paneled triptychs with broken ceramics, fabric pieces, paint, paper and wood during meditation and music. Again, enthusiasm welled up from the participants.

The experience branded an impression on my heart. Art lit a fire in the participants' bones to enhance feelings, to give them insight and boldness to create with their hands. They ably brought down images from their free-roaming musings and captured them in their art work. Art had snared and gripped them. Through the retreat, the women poured their souls into their work, which vibrated there on the work tables as each of us shared what we had created.

Decidedly I must champion this powerful process. My art must overflow in this direction. I would not offer or accept leading any more events of any kind unless I could include making art.

## Visual Art in Worship

By following my bliss, doors continued to swing open. St Andrews Presbyterian Church's membership contained a group of artists who created artistic embellishments for worship. The pastor recognized that they needed guidance and he called me. I happily responded with a resounding "Of course!" I left Columbia Church when its minister left, and the door opened for me to connect with St. Andrews.

The group of artists at St. Andrews consisted of six women who created art in painting, quilting, needlework, and stained glass. I initially led the group through a discussion on the place of art in the church which, I asserted, must remain open-ended and not directed toward a specific end. ("No words on banners for me," I said.) Like parables, such visual expression lies dangerously open to misinterpretation. But viewers become more engaged by drawing their own conclusions, I assured the group. After some discussion we considered how to express the themes of worship in the sanctuary. We called ourselves the Liturgical Arts Team and met monthly.

Our efforts began with red enhanced designs for Pentecost. In the Fall, we focused on Advent. To stimulate deep thinking about Advent, I started out by unpacking the statement: "The arts incarnate our experience of mystery, wonder and awe, and enable us to encounter the Holy."

"Do any of us here ever come closer to God through the arts?" I asked. "If so, how? How can we get others to encounter mystery and awe during Advent through our liturgical arts?" I linked the questions with readings from Isaiah and the Gospel accounts of the Nativity. I challenged them to consider their feelings about Advent. Then I asked, what of our feelings do we want to convey to the congregation? Chewing on the readings and my questions, feelings and phrases spilled out among the group.

"Needing hope," said Margaret.

"Expectation," chimed in Penny.

"Waiting," said Connie.

"Promise," called out Marianne.

"Being ready," said Stell.

"Light versus darkness," said Carole.

Energy mounted as one person after another contributed. By tapping into the women's observations and feelings, ideas for art in Advent grew beyond any of mine. I didn't have to push and pull to force a direction to follow or blatantly tell them what to do. My introductions and gentle questions triggered a heartfelt response from the group. They carried the burden and the joy of creating something for worship. By delving deeper into the meaning of Advent, each of them tapped into their souls out of which emerged art which truly communicated. They felt empowered to make the art. I, too, felt empowered that I had successfully navigated them through the creative process to devise their own plan. I was exhilarated beyond measure.

In the process, we scoured our minds and imaginations over the course of several Sunday meetings to implement our Advent themes. With the depth and number of feelings expressed, one person said with some exasperation, "How can we express it all?" To encompass the range of feelings, images and ideas, we created one on-going banner to which additions were made for each of the four Sundays leading to Christmas. Each Sunday followed the theme of the Advent hymn, *People, Look East*, with images of house, bird, flowering plant and star. After Advent, we loaned the hanging to a nearby Methodist church. When they had used it for Advent the following year, a member wrote: "Thank you for sharing this beautiful piece of art that added so much to our worship.... Many comments were made about its beauty and meaning."

I wondered if the group's enthusiasm would wane until the next church season but happily it did not. We decided to work on something for Ordinary Time which usually extends from June to December. Once more I immersed the women with thoughts and feelings concerning spiritual growth, the major theme of the season. We mused over the image of the vine in John 15. In order to support this theme, we again created an ongoing four-week design for the sanctuary, this time for the summer. We *grew* vines on successive Sundays, starting with naked branches, then leaves, flowers followed by fruit and wove them in and out of the cross on the central grill that covered the pipes of the organ. Sermons and music on Scriptural vines expanded the theme. When we took it all down, leaving the sanctuary bare once more, one member said, "I miss the vine. I guess someone forgot to water it!"

...

I offered a one-day retreat for the Team, calling it *Imaging our Faith: A Retreat in Creativity and Art Making.* My amazement grew when on a Saturday the whole team plus a few others trooped into the church fellowship hall for the retreat. I found a way to work around resistances so no participant would bolt because of fear as in my previous church. I bypassed their reservations by saying we were to make *visual representations* of their responses, not artistic renditions. I witnessed them plunge into the activities with gusto. They shaped clay to respond to the Jeremiah passage of Scripture (18:1-6) about God the potter and humankind the clay; painted wet-on-wet water color to mirror the lack of control on the stormy Sea of Galilee (Mark 4:35-41); they created collages and white pencil drawings on black paper, responding to other scripture passages. The women affirmed the retreat in heart-warming ways. Tears, laughter, sober thoughts, deep sharing, and new visions clustered among them.

As a result of the retreat the minister asked me to become intentionally related to the congregation in an arts capacity. I was called Parish Associate for Arts Ministry and was able to encourage art making in St. Andrews in ways I was not able to in Columbia Church.

## Exhibiting My Quilts

While I facilitated art in the churches, an arts and cultural group in Brunswick, Georgia invited artists to exhibit in a juried sacred art exhibition. With hesitation, I submitted slides of the *Transformation* quilt. I could not contain my excitement when it was accepted. Pete and I made the five-hour trip to the opening night for the event. I jumped when I saw my quilt hanging among other works of art. My joy overflowed.

A friend who had exhibited her photography in other venues accompanied us to the exhibit. When we ate together afterward, she said softly to me, "You know, my husband has never come to any of my exhibits." I winced. I knew what a treasure I had in Pete's support. He had come a long way with me on my journey into art. When we later moved into our new house in North Carolina he heard me speak to a seniors group about my quilts. He was astonished. He had never heard the stories behind all the quilts or how I composed them. Upon returning home, he moved furniture around to create a *headquarters* — a studio for me, complete with an installed skylight.

For five years, every successive art exhibit in Brunswick accepted a quilt of mine. I also entered *Why Not Become All Flame?* into a juried sacred art exhibition at Concordia Theological Seminary in Austin, Texas. In the summer of 2001, all seven of my quilts hung in exhibits: in Brunswick, in the Sacred Threads exhibit in Columbus, Ohio, in the Virginia Quilt Museum, and in a Black Mountain quilt shop. My dream to exhibit my work had unfolded beyond my wildest expectations. Through these exhibitions I shared my art with the widest assortment of viewers. I began to regard exhibitions of my work as part of my ministry of proclaiming the Good News visually, not just verbally.

The supreme opportunity for showing my quilts occurred for four months in 2011 when my Seminary, Columbia, exhibited 18 pieces of my work. The show was called *Inspiration: Spiritual Dimensions of Fabric Art.* My framed artist's statement plus titles for each piece connected spirituality and art. Roaming the halls of the Continuing Education Center, students, faculty, staff, trustees, visitors and ministers viewed the art quilts on its walls as objects of interest, curiosity, and also as vehicles for contemplation. A few of the viewers related to me their excitement of seeing my work especially as an alumna of the Seminary who had found her artistic niche. Some individuals who saw my work made arrangements for another seminary to hang the quilts in an exhibition. So in August, nine of the pieces were sent to Austin Presbyterian Seminary in Texas, another meaningful venue to host my work. I could hardly contain my joy over the wide reception of my creations, especially in a theological setting. Perhaps, too, with these exhibitions, I contributed in a small way to an increased understanding of how art readily enhances our faith.

■ ■ ■

More and more, my art has overflowed through teaching and leading in workshops and retreats in church and conference venues. Titles of a few include *Telling Your Story Visually*, *Imaging Our Inner Treasure*, *A Visual Lectio Divina*, *Contemplative Seeing*, *and Praying Visually*. The high point in my teaching came when I co-led an art and spirituality course for my Seminary. I lectured on the didactic material concerning the place of art and creativity in the life of the church. Topics included: What Happened to Art in the Church, and Why We Need It, Incarnated Spirituality, and Creation and Creativity. Lynne Farrow, artist and spiritual guide from California, led the fifteen women in studio time in the afternoons to make journals and expressive paintings.

Again, I reveled in watching art making catch fire. Most of the participants came with heavy reservations about art. "I'm not creative," or "A paint brush and blank paper terrifies me," we heard at the beginning. In her introductions, Lynne distributed a quote by an anonymous author to the group: "Everything we do in life we do before God alone, and to the glory of God alone, and with the view of pleasing God alone — the Audience of One." Participants immediately relaxed in a newfound freedom. One person said, "That pointed me into a new direction: toward God and not toward others' views." She said the week had been the most meaningful experience she had ever had..."like a new birthday, a new beginning."

When the participants returned home, one began an art group in her church.

Another introduced visual art and praying with icons to her youth group. A hospital chaplain encouraged watercolor painting with her patients and found they opened up more easily while painting. Several bought art supplies and carved out spaces in their homes for a tiny studio. Others, in sharing their art back home experienced reconciliation with family members.

The women's creative expressions and enthusiasm blossomed right under my eyes. I thrilled to see participants face their fears, take courage by the hand, and welcome new potentials into their lives. I particularly relished the fact that Lynne's and my facilitation flowed into new pockets of need through the fifteen women's new artistic efforts.

## My Artist's Statement

Clearly, the overflow of my art confirmed my vocation as an artist. I expressed my beliefs about my newfound ministry in an artist's statement:

> Although I am a minister of the Word and Sacrament in the Presbyterian Church (USA), I am discovering more and more the power of non-verbal language. I view my art making as a form of ministry ... to proclaim the Good News of the Gospel visually...I hope that my fiber pieces evoke from viewers an experience of joy, wonder and goodness about life, and about God. Some people of faith feed hungry bodies in the name of Christ; my deepest desire is to feed hungry spirits through art.

I went on to say how I create quilts from intuition, with no pre-conceived plan, which requires a process of discernment — of waiting and listening. Improvisation lies at the heart of my art making, of launching out not knowing the way initially. I also stated that art is a contemplative experience for me, creating something in solitude that can be shared with the larger community for the glory of God.

I ended with: "Art is healing for me. It brings me vitality and passion. I must do it in order to take a step toward wholeness for myself. I am awed and grateful every time I am involved in an art piece, from beginning to completion. In the creative process, I experience something of God."

## My Art in a New Environment

In retirement we moved to the quiet mountains of western North Carolina. I discovered that I had landed in a field so fertile that my artistic seeds could amply sprout and grow. Growing an art ministry while in Atlanta was restricted to church settings, with little other opportunity to display my quilts, talk about them or lead workshops. In the Black Mountain, Montreat and Asheville areas, however, door after door has opened to share my quilts and discuss my creative process: in church gatherings, retirement homes, in community and conference centers, in libraries, in art and quilt guilds, and in Asheville's North Carolina Arboretum. I have led more art retreats and workshops plus encouraged new and experienced artists as they and I pursued *The Artist's Way*. I helped initiate an Arts Council in the Montreat Conference Center where we introduced exhibits, conferences and newsletters in order to expose Presbyterian conferees to the power of art in worship and faith.

I have also wanted to address social disruptions with the healing power of art. Manifold opportunities dot my environment: with cancer survivors, hospice patients, prisoners, struggling adolescents or various marginalized people. A call to resist the status quo through art sounded when I heard a penetrating story which burrowed into my heart. During the Bosnian War in the 1990's, Sarajevo came under siege by Serb snipers on the high mountains surrounding the city. One afternoon in 1992 an urgency to buy food brought hungry people out of their homes to stand in a bread line. While they waited, a sniper fired down upon them and killed twenty-two people. The town was overwhelmed with horror, anger and grief.

The next day, Smailovic Vedran, the principal cellist in the Sarajevo opera theater, came out dressed in black as for a concert. He brought his cello and a fire-charred chair to the spot where the twenty-two had fallen, sat down and began to play the mournful notes of Albinoni's Adagio in G Minor for cello. He did this every day for 22 days. Through his music he brought consolation, hope and defiance against violence and war. Soon, other musicians joined him. Today, a bronze statue of a man playing a cello sits in the main square of Sarajevo. Smailovic is honored all over the world.

When I heard it, the story brought tears to my eyes. As a result, I perceived a call to bring my art to some place of pain, grief or disruption. Through making art, displaying my quilts plus leading others into artistic ventures, I want to offer healing, empowerment and hope. After deep pondering, I believe the chief issue I wish to address is the abuse and destruction of the environment. Grief engulfs me frequently when I hear about pollution, the demise of life forms, and the overshadowing of earth's beauty with human ignorance, indifference and greed. I keep mulling over possible depictions for this effort and will begin work with the completion of this book.

## African Overflow

One issue I have addressed is the widespread tragic trauma of the AIDS pandemic in Africa. Beginning a quilt with African themes and patterns, I chose fabrics which gleamed in luscious tones of brown, rust, gold and bronze, two of which I hand painted. Constructing small pieces, I gained inspiration from a book of African designs. I delighted in cutting shapes from South African hand-printed fabric donated by my friend Connie, and a worn piece of Ghanaian *kente* cloth. I cut out *adinkra* symbols from Ghanaian culture imprinted on commercial fabric from my stash. Other designs emerged from Maasai and Zulu warrior shields, a Nigerian gourd, and Congolese *bakuba* cloth. I puzzled over which fabric could serve as background to tie everything together. I rifled through my drawers of African cloth. A rather busy print from Ghana that we had used as a curtain grabbed my attention. Containing most of the colors found in the small pieces, it tied everything together beautifully. I cut out geometric shapes of bright aqua to dot here and there on the quilt to give pizazz. I fastened the shapes by hand, along with a string of waist beads from West Africa. Among our collection of African artifacts, I found anklets of seeds which jangle in dancing — a perfect use for them in the quilt. Eventually, I discerned a sense of direction before layering the pieces into the quilt. To broaden my skills, I quilted the piece by machine. I drew no pattern on the top fabric for stitching but just spontaneously started in an intricate pattern of inter-connecting lines and squares. The improvisational quilting proved challenging, but I persevered. Step by step, it all came together.

A name for the quilt eluded me for awhile. Its components seemed to frolic before my eyes in an unrestrained African dance. Drumbeats almost sounded in my ears. Yet, I was aware of the deep sorrow on the continent because of AIDS. I also knew that Africans danced both in their joy and in their grief. So I called the quilt *You Have Turned My Mourning into Dancing*, from Psalm 30:11. I am hoping indeed that some day Africans will dance more from joy than from grieving. I dedicated the quilt to the survivors of AIDS.

Two quilts of mine now contain African artifacts and designs. As I plumb the depths of what it meant to live in West Africa all those years, I yearn to express how my sojourn there has impacted my life. Perhaps my quilts derived from African fabrics might create an alternative view not only of a way of life but also of the continent. Already, one friend has said of the *Transformation* quilt, "You know, we hear so much negative stuff about Africa: disease, poverty, conflicts. But in this quilt, you have shown a positive, joyous side. Keep it up!"

My considerable collection of African prints beckons to me to continue to bring the people of that misnamed "dark" continent into light and to express their vitality and beauty. An acquaintance in Ghana sewed two long Ghanaian two-piece dresses for me, one of a tie-dye tan and blue, the other a lively indigo blue print with bold borders. A commercial print of cream and aqua made into a dress which I loved lies unused. Too small for me now, they all live in my drawer along with two *dashikis* Pete once wore. Former curtains and chair coverings from Ghana and Nigeria along with the once-worn clothing insist on inclusion in future quilts. The exuberance and wildly merging colors and patterns of the fabrics claim my attention. They call out "Don't forget us.

Use us! Bring us to light! Make us visible to the world."

I intend to respond to their call. Then my overflow will have stretched beyond North Carolina, beyond our shores, and far beyond my dreams.

**YOU HAVE TURNED MY MOURNING INTO DANCING**
36 x 27"

*"The wild colors in my African fabrics cry out 'Bring us to the light! Make us visible to the world!'"*

# 12
## MYSTERY AND WONDER:
## REFLECTIONS

❧❦

I sit in silence in the chapel of Green Bough House of Prayer in the heart of Georgia. Daylight barely illumines the room. Within a few minutes, sky hues of pale pink and mauve paint the wall behind the communion table. They herald the glorious dawn that soon turns ripples of clouds into blazing pink and gold, and kindles a stirring in my heart. The advancing sunlight overcomes the humble candle flame on the table. I swell with joy to be alive, to be able to see, to be able to soak in and clasp to my breast the mystery, wonder, and glorious beauty of God. I smile as I warm my hands on the mug of tea I have brought with me into the space. Through the window I contemplate the bare trees which seem ignited by the flaming sky. They seem to burn and glow with an inner radiance, like a burning bush from where God calls my name and commissions me. I smile because of the mystery, wonder and extravagant *grace* of God who embraces me and who has called me. Gratitude overcomes me.

Like Moses at the burning bush, like Elijah in the cave, like Peter at his fishing boat, we followers of Christ are called to various missions. I look back at the variety of calls I responded to: nursing, overseas mission work, wife and mother, writer, spiritual guide, ordained minister and finally artist. I can only affirm the notion by Elizabeth O'Connor that different stages of life open doors to different callings. As I review the convoluted paths and rabbit trails I took before welcoming this call into art, I am amazed. Amazed that the call to make art simply waited in the wings until I was ready to embrace it. Amazed that questions and doubts did not lasso me and throw me to the ground. Amazed that my ministry in art has been affirmed by others and has born fruit in soul-stirring ways.

Who would have thought the improvisations of my life would bring me to this present sense of joyful fulfillment, built on all the previous calls and roles I have assumed over the years? Wearing an assortment of hats even today I often wonder, *Who am I? What have I to show for my endeavors?* My answer parallels that of M.C. Richards when asked, "What do you do"? Whether to answer teacher, poet or potter, she answered, "Person." Ignoring others' expectations and delving into one role after another, she thought something was wrong with her, "always on the march... from landscape to landscape," but striving fully to be who she was: a person of multiple capacities.

This book, too, marches from landscape to landscape. It straddles many topics and concerns, chiefly art making, spirituality, discernment, ministry and writing. It reflects who I am, a conglomerate person, trying to hold together all these disparate and passionate interests and abilities. Other people tend to laud multi-gifted persons. I find it can be an affliction with its push-pull dimensions, spilling me out all over the place and obscuring a focus on one thing at a time. If anything ties my roles, gifts and call together I would say it is as a Proclaimer: sharing the Good News of God's personal care and love to whoever hears me or sees my art or reads my work. Through teaching, preaching, writing and art making, I am a Proclaimer actively working to communicate God's fiery presence in my life and in the community around me. Improvisation clarifies the form of proclamation I am to assume at a given time, which gift to concentrate on, which direction to go. It teaches me to revel in the gifts and passions each day offers up. Go where vibrancy flows. Delight in the textured richness of a complex life. Rely on intuition and a sense of a right direction pointing the way out of multiple possibilities. I recall: "You take a step. You pay attention. You decide which way to go for the next step."

For me, a sense of energy, excitement and passion has guided me, not only in creating art quilts but in creating my life. I believe God used these elements to propel me toward each step at just the right time.

I recall the events and people who directed me and supported my call. *New Pieces Quilt Shop*. Nancy Chinn. Joseph Campbell. Bezalel. Nena Bryans. Ghost Ranch. Cathy Kapikian. Hildegard of Bingen. Legion of Mark Five. Ignatius of Loyola. Art teacher Mrs. Graham. Thomas Merton. *The Artist's Way*. Vedran Smailovic. What disparate pieces of a puzzle! Like dangling, glittering gems strung from a mobile, dancing around, catching light, instilling awe, and shaping my artistic sensibility. A life-giving collection reflecting the myriad, creative even subversive ways in which God has given guidance. Who would have thought that, after a wondrous and rich six decades of journeying, God would crown me with the vitality and exuberance I experience through art in my seventh decade?

### ● ● ●

A few years ago, I began a piece with very diverse components. I joined a workshop in Taos, New Mexico on creativity, designed mainly for those making wearable art. Perhaps this different focus of the participants pushed me into a new direction. I began two new fiber pieces, not quilts by definition, since the pieces contained irregular layers, no batting, and minimal hand stitching to hold everything together. From then on, I would make fiber art, freely composing from one step to another as energy led me within or outside the confines of a quilt.

In one piece I hand stitched small panels from disassembled Guatemalan purses mounted with two large metal beads on a piece of hand painted fabric. I placed this on a triangular piece of black at the bottom of which I sewed a luminous flower taken from a decorator swatch. Behind it lay a wine colored print on which I discharged (bleached) a random pattern. All of this was sewn on a fabric panel of sienna colored leaves which was also mounted on a panel depicting swirling grass. Tabs of the discharged fabric held the stick for mounting. I called it *Promise and Fulfillment*.

In another many-layered creation, on a torn piece of Hmong cross stitch, I sewed a large, striking button, and a tangle of threads pulled from the raw edges of fabric. Behind this, the layers included a green raw silk splashed with gold paint, a barely visible piece of red silk, and a tie-dyed gold, tan and pink piece from a skirt our daughter wore in Ghana. The collection was attached to different panels of brown with four rows of large stitches. I hung the piece from a knobby stick with colorful threads to hang it and also to dangle down with beads on their knotted ends. I called it *Recollection*, which represented the contents of the quilt. It is also a word used to center oneself, a process in which we recollect all the scattered parts of ourselves in order to pray. The piece additionally represented my recollection of the experiences and contacts that have made me come alive along my journey into art.

■ ■ ■

As I consider the mystery of my journey into art, I believe that passion as I first experienced it in *New Pieces* has given me the most direct sense of guidance in both my life and my art. Just as *passion* has guided me in quilt making so it has pointed the way for me to go. My quilts have taught me to recognize the same passionate *Yes!* in my desire to call myself an artist. I eventually realized that creating art was God's will, God's longing and mission for me: to smile, to contribute, to be fulfilled, to come alive as I image my inner fire.

Still, creating art never seems easy to do. In these pages I have shared the obstacles and challenges I have encountered in bringing life to my gift. No matter how far along this journey I have traveled, I constantly find myself a beginner in art making. I must seek and listen to direction. Every project is new, every art piece harbors its own resistances that I have to overcome or work around. Courage must whisper in my ear, "Yes, you can do it!" from start to finish. Then when the new thing is complete I call on Courage again, this time to walk with me as I carry it beyond my work space into the wider world.

I share my work with others because I really do not own my gift nor am I the author of it. I am simply the grateful bearer and steward of the gift, and participate in its mystery. My responsibility towards this gift is to nurture it so that out of it my best efforts will flow outward to others. God has called me with my gifts not just for my sake, but for the life of the world. In order to continue the creation of the world, I am called to use my gifts in co-creating with God for the common good. I therefore cannot withhold what I have been empowered to create. I cannot stand forever on the brink, hesitant, cautious, fearful. The world will not have my song unless I sing it. A paraphrase of Dag Hammarskjold, Swedish diplomat and second Secretary-General of the UN reflects my journey into art: "You take the pen — and the lines dance. You take the flute — and the notes shimmer. You take the brush — and the colors sing. So all things have meaning and beauty in that space beyond time where You are. How, then, can I hold back anything from You?"

*Yes!*

**RECOLLECTION**
23.5 xx 16.5"

*"The very diverse components of the hanging pictured the assemblage of myself."*

Audette, Anna Held, *The Blank Canvas: Inviting the Muse*, Boston and London: Shambhala, 1993.

Barlow, Margaret, *Women Artists*, Hong Kong: Hugh Lauter Levin Associates, 1999.

Bateson, Mary Catherine, *Composing a Life*, New York: Penguin Books, 1989.

Beckett, Sister Wendy, *Sister Wendy on Prayer*, New York: Harmony Books (an imprint of the Crown Publishing Group, a Division of Random House, Inc.), 2006.

Benke, Britta, *Georgia O'Keeffe, 1887-1986: Flowers in the Desert*, New York: Barnes and Noble Books, 2001.

Bryans, Nena, *Full Circle: A Proposal to the Church for an Arts Ministry*, San Carlo, CA: Schuyler Institute for Worship and the Arts, 1988.

Campbell, Joseph, *The Power of Myth* with Bill Moyers, New York: Doubleday, 1988.

Caprio, Betsy, Thomas M. Hedberg, *Coming Home: A Manual for Spiritual Direction*, New York: Paulist Press, 1986.

Chicago, Judy, *Beyond the Flower: The Autobiography of a Feminist Artist*, New York: Penguin Books, 1996.

Clarke, John, trans., *Story of a Soul: The Autobiography of St. Thérèse of Lisieux*. Washington, DC: ICS Publications, 1975.

Csikszentmihalyi, Mihaly, *Creativity: Flow and the Psychology of Discovery and Invention*. New York: HarperCollins, 1996.

De Chardin, Pierre Teilhard, *Hymn of the Universe*, New York: Harper and Row Publishers, Inc. 1965.

De Waal, Esther, *A World Made Whole: Rediscovering the Celtic Tradition*, London: Fount, An Imprint of HarperCollins, Publishers. 1991.

Division of Christian Education of the National Council of Churches of Christ in the United States of America, *The Holy Bible: New Revised Standard Version*. New York: Oxford University Press, 1989.

Estes, Clarissa Pinkola, *Women Who Run with the Wolves: Myths and Stories of the Wild Woman Archetype*, New York: Ballantine Books, 1992.

Farnham, Suzanne G., Joseph P. Gill, R.Taylor McLean, Susan M. Ward, *Listening Hearts: Discerning Call in Community*. Harrisburg, PA: Morehouse Publishing, 1991.

Fleming, David L., ed. *Modern Spiritual Exercises: a Contemporary Reading of the Spiritual Exercises of St. Ignatius*, Garden City, New York: Image Books, a Division of Doubleday and Company. 1983.

Hammarskjold, Dag, *Markings*, New York: Alfred A. Knopf, 1964.

Herrera, Hayden, *Frieda Kahlo*, New York: Rizzoli Art Series, 1992.

Hildegard of Bingen (Robert Carver, trans.), *Mystical Writings*, Fiona Bowie and Oliver Davis, eds. New York: Crossroad, 1990.

Judson, Sylvia, *The Quiet Eye: A Way of Looking at Pictures*, Washington DC: Regnery Publishing, 1954.

Kearns, Martha, *Kathe Kollwitz: Woman and Artist*. New York: The Feminist Press at the City University of New York, 1976.

Kettenmann, Andrea, *Frieda Kahlo, 1907-1954, Pain and Passion*, Koln, Germany: Taschen, 2000.

Kidd, Sue Monk, *The Dance of the Dissident Daughter: A Woman's Journey from Christian Tradition to the Sacred Feminine*, Harper San Francisco, 1996.

Lamott, Anne, *Bird by Bird: Some Instructions on Writing and Life*, New York: Doubleday, 1994.

Maisel, Eric, *Fearless Creating: A Step-by-Step Guide to Starting and Completing Your Work of Art*, New York: Jeremy P. Tarcher / Putnam Books, 1995.

*Merriam-Webster's Collegiate Dictionary*, 10th edition, Springfield, Massachusetts: Merriam Company, Incorporated, 1993.

Merton, Thomas, *Dialogues with Silence: Prayers and Drawings*, Harper San Francisco: 2001.

Ibid, *New Seeds of Contemplation*, New York: A New Directions Book, 1961.

Ibid, *Thoughts in Solitude*, New York: Farrar, Straus and Giroux, 1958.

Miles, Margaret R., *Image as Insight: Visual Understanding in Western Christianity*, Boston: Beacon Press, 1985.

O'Connor, Elizabeth. *The Eighth Day of Creation: Discovering Your Gifts and Using Them*, Waco TX: Word Books, 1971.

O'Connor, Flannery, *Mystery and Manners: Occasional Prose*, edited by Sally and Robert Fitzgerald. New York: Farrar, Straus and Giroux, 1969.

O'Keeffe, Georgia, *Some Memories of Drawings*, Albuquerque: the University of New Mexico Press, 1988.

Piepenburg, Robert, *Treasures of the Creative Spirit: An Artist's Understanding of Human Creativity*, Farmington Hills, MI: Pebble Press Inc., 1998.

*The Presbyterian Hymnal, Spirit of God, Descend upon my Heart*, Louisville: Westminster/John Knox Press, 1990.

Ibid, *We Give Thee But Thine Own*.

Ibid, *The Lone Wild Bird*.

Richards, M.C., *Centering in Pottery, Poetry and the Person*, Middletown, CN: Wesleyan University Press, 1989.

Rilke, Rainier Maria, (Trans. M.D. Herter Norton), *Letters to a Young Poet*, New York: W.W. Norton and Company, Inc., 1963.

Rock, Judith, quoted in Nena Bryans, *Full Circle: A Proposal to the Church for an Arts Ministry*, San Carlo, CA: Schuyler Institute for Worship and the Arts, 1988.

Tagore, Rabindrinath, *Show Yourself to My Soul*, Notre Dame: Sorin Books, 2002.

Underhill, Evelyn, *Mysticism: A Study in the Nature and Development of Spiritual Consciousness*, Mineola, New York: Dover Publications, 2002.

Ward, Benedicta, ed., *The Desert Christian: The Sayings of the Desert Fathers*, New York: Macmillan, 1980.

The persons in this list offered enormous support to me and help along the way as I wrote this book, either through encouragement and/or offering advice when they had read the manuscript:

Sue Lile Inman, Roberta Parker Martin, Jeanette Stokes, Gretchen Campbell, Loretta McCarthy, Nancy Chinn, Nena Bryans, Cathy Kapikian, Brian Mahan and Kim Boykin, Mary and Kent Logan, Connie Conrad, Irene Prokopf, Fay Key, Sara Covin Juengst, Peggy Tabor Millin, Chris McMillan, Helen N. Johnson, Paula Huston, Luci Shaw, Barbara Earnhardt, C.D. Weaver, Jeanie Franklin, Judith Toy, Ellen Philips, Sister Peggy Verstege, Greta Reed, Virginia Bethune, Dick and Lila Ray, Ina Hughs and Roberta Binder.

At the request of friends I am listing workshops and classes in art and in writing which I attended:

FABRIC ART:

New Pieces Quilt Shop, Berkeley CA: "Log Cabin with a Twist," Sandi Cumming, April 1993.
Penland School of Craft, NC: "Quilt Making," Terri Hancock, June 1996.
Grunewald Guild, Leavenworth, WA: "Fabric and Color," Larkin van Horn, July 2000.
Arrowmont School of Arts and Crafts, Gatlinburg TN: "The Art Quilt: Painting and Composition," Natasha Kempers-Cullen, June 2001.
Yarns to Dye For, Hendersonville, NC, "Painting on Silk," Donna Kassab, May 2002.
Design Outside the Lines, Taos NM: "Creativity, Fiber and Sewing Retreat," Diane Ericson and Marcy Tilton, September 2003.
Fiber Arts Alliance, Black Mountain NC: "Surface Design Sampler," Jeanne Rafer Beck, October 2006.
Cloth, Asheville, NC: "Inspired by Nature: Art Quilts," Norma Bradley, July 2008.
Cloth, Asheville, NC: "Shibori and Indigo," Eileen Hallman, May 2009.
Cloth, Asheville, NC: "Print, Collage, Stitch," Bernie Rowell, October 2010
Montreat Conference Center, NC: "Silkscreen Print Making," Louise Cecil, July 2012

WRITING:

Clarity Works, Asheville, NC: Peggy Tabor Millin, one-on-one mentoring, 2004-2006.
The Mid-Atlantic Creative Non-Fiction Conference, Goucher College, Towson MD: August 2005.
The Glen Workshop, sponsored by *Image*, Santa Fe, NM: Paula Huston, July 2007.

**WORKSHOPS AND RETREATS:**

In addition to creating her art quilts, various wall hangings, and collages with fabric and paper, Martha Jane leads: weekend, five-day and one-day workshops and retreats, combining spiritual practices with art making. For more information, she can be reached at: 301 Allen Mountain Drive, Black Mountain, NC 28711, 828-669-3945 or through her website www.MarthaJanePetersen.com.